APR. 04

Forensic Examination of Digital Evidence: A Guide for Law Enforcement

NCJ 199408

Sarah V. Hart
Director

This document was prepared under Interagency Agreement #1999–IJ–R–094 between the National Institute of Justice and the National Institute of Standards and Technology, Office of Law Enforcement Standards.

The National Institute of Justice is a component of the Office of Justice Programs, which also includes the Bureau of Justice Assistance, the Bureau of Justice Statistics, the Office of Juvenile Justice and Delinquency Prevention, and the Office for Victims of Crime.

Foreword

Developments in the world have shown how simple it is to acquire all sorts of information through the use of computers. This information can be used for a variety of endeavors, and criminal activity is a major one. In an effort to fight this new crime wave, law enforcement agencies, financial institutions, and investment firms are incorporating computer forensics into their infrastructure. From network security breaches to child pornography investigations, the common bridge is the demonstration that the particular electronic media contained the incriminating evidence. Supportive examination procedures and protocols should be in place in order to show that the electronic media contains the incriminating evidence.

To assist law enforcement agencies and prosecutorial offices, a series of guides dealing with digital evidence has been selected to address the complete investigation process. This process expands from the crime scene through analysis and finally into the courtroom. The guides summarize information from a select group of practitioners who are knowledgeable about the subject matter. These groups are more commonly known as technical working groups.

This guide is the second in a series. The first guide, *Electronic Crime Scene Investigation: A Guide for First Responders*, is available through the National Institute of Justice Web site at http://www.ojp.usdoj.gov/nij/pubs-sum/187736.htm.

The remaining guides in the series will address—

- Using high technology to investigate.

- Investigating high technology crimes.

- Creating a digital evidence forensic unit.

- Presenting digital evidence in the courtroom.

Because of the complex issues associated with digital evidence examination, the Technical Working Group for the Examination of Digital Evidence (TWGEDE) recognized that its recommendations may not be feasible in all circumstances. The guide's recommendations are not legal mandates or policy directives, nor do they represent the *only* correct courses of action. Rather, the recommendations represent a consensus of the diverse views and experiences of the technical working group members who have provided valuable insight into these important issues. The National Institute of Justice (NIJ) expects that each jurisdiction will be able to use these recommendations to spark discussions and ensure that its practices and procedures are best suited to its unique environment.

It is our hope that, through these materials, more of our Nation's law enforcement personnel will be trained to work effectively with digital evidence and maximize the reliability of that evidence to the benefit of criminal case prosecutions.

NIJ extends its appreciation to the participants in the TWGEDE for their dedication to the preparation of this guide. Their efforts are particularly commendable given that they were not relieved of their existing duties with their home offices or agencies while they participated in the TWGEDE. What is more, it was necessary for

TWGEDE members to attend numerous (and lengthy) guide preparation meetings that were held at locations far removed from their home offices or agencies. In recognition of this, NIJ expresses great appreciation for the commitment made by the home offices or agencies of TWGEDE members in suffering the periodic unavailability of their employees.

Sarah V. Hart
Director
National Institute of Justice

Technical Working Group for the Examination of Digital Evidence

The process of developing the guide was initiated through an invitational process. Invitees for the Technical Working Group for the Examination of Digital Evidence (TWGEDE) were selected initially for their expertise with digital evidence and then by their profession. The intent was to incorporate a medley of individuals with law enforcement, corporate, or legal affiliations to ensure a complete representation of the communities involved with digital evidence.

A small core of individuals was invited to comprise the planning panel. The task of the planning panel was to formulate a basic outline of topics that would be considered for inclusion.

NIJ thanks Michael P. Everitt of the U.S. Postal Service, Office of Inspector General, and Michael J. Menz. Both of these individuals provided their invaluable time and expertise during the guide's review process.

Planning panel

Susan Ballou
Program Manager, Forensic Science
Office of Law Enforcement Standards
National Institute of Standards and
  Technology
Gaithersburg, Maryland

Kenneth Broderick
Special Agent
U.S. Bureau of Alcohol, Tobacco,
  Firearms and Explosives
Computer Forensics Branch
Sterling, Virginia

Charles J. Faulk
Special Agent
U.S. Bureau of Alcohol, Tobacco,
  Firearms and Explosives
Portland, Oregon

Grant Gottfried
Senior Specialist
National Center for Forensic Science
Orlando, Florida

Kim Herd
Criminal Law and Technology Counsel
National Association of Attorneys General
Washington, D.C.

Mark Johnson
Sergeant
Computer Crimes Unit
Kansas City, Missouri, Police
Kansas City, Missouri

Michael McCartney
Investigator
New York State Attorney General's Office
Criminal Prosecution Bureau–Organized
  Crime Task Force
Buffalo, New York

Mark Menz
Digital Evidence Scientist
Folsom, California

Bill Moylan
Detective
Nassau County Police Department
Computer Crime Section
Crimes Against Property Squad
Westbury, New York

Glenn Nick
Assistant Director
U.S. Customs Service
Cyber Smuggling Center
Fairfax, Virginia

Todd Shipley
Detective Sergeant
Reno Police Department
Computer Crimes Unit
Reno, Nevada

Andy Siske
Defense Computer Investigation Training
  Program
Linthicum, Maryland

Chris Stippich
Digital Intelligence, Inc.
Waukesha, Wisconsin

TWGEDE members

Additional members were then incorporated into the TWGEDE to provide a full technical working group. The individuals listed below, along with the planning panel, worked together to formulate this guide.

Abigail Abraham
Assistant State's Attorney
Cook County State's Attorney's Office
Chicago, Illinois

Chris G. Andrist
Agent
Colorado Bureau of Investigation
Denver, Colorado

Sean Barry
Computer Forensics Assistant Lab
  Manager
New Technologies, Inc.
Gresham, Oregon

Bill Baugh
CEO
Savannah Technology Group
Savannah, Georgia

Randy Bishop
Special Agent in Charge
U.S. Department of Energy
Office of Inspector General
Technology Crime Section
Washington, D.C.

Carleton Bryant
Staff Attorney
Knox County Sheriff's Office
Knoxville, Tennessee

Don Buchwald
Project Engineer
The Aerospace Corporation
Los Angeles, California

Jaime Carazo
Special Agent
United States Secret Service
Electronic Crimes Branch
Washington, D.C.

Keith G. Chval
Chief, High Tech Crimes Bureau
Office of the Illinois Attorney General
Chicago, Illinois

Dorothy E. Denning
Professor
Computer Science Department
Georgetown University
Washington, D.C.

Dan Dorman
Inspector
Postal Inspection Service
Atlanta, Georgia

James Doyle
Sergeant
Detective Bureau
New York City Police Department
Computer Investigation and Technology
  Unit
New York, New York

Michael Duncan
Staff/Sergeant
Economic Crime Branch
Technological Crime Section
Ottawa, Ontario
Canada

Doug Elrick
Senior Forensic Specialist
Digital Intelligence
Waukesha, Wisconsin

Michael Finnie
Forensic Specialist
Computer Forensics Inc.
Seattle, Washington

Toby M. Finnie
Director
High Tech Crime Consortium
Tacoma, Washington

Paul T. French
Director, Consulting Services
New Technologies, Inc.
Computer Forensics Lab Manager
Gresham, Oregon

Pat Gilmore
Director
RedSiren, Inc.
Pittsburgh, Pennsylvania

Sam Guttman
Postal Inspector
Forensic and Technical Services
U.S. Postal Service
Dulles, Virginia

Dave Heslep
Sergeant
Maryland State Police
Computer Forensics Laboratory
Columbia, Maryland

Al Hobbs
Special Deputy U.S. Marshal
Child Exploitation Strike Force
Arlington Heights Police Department
Arlington Heights, Illinois

Robert Hopper
Sergeant
Arizona Department of Public Safety
Computer Forensic Unit
Phoenix, Arizona

Mary Horvath
Program Manager
FBI–CART
Washington, D.C.

Nigel Jones
Programme Manager
National High Tech Crime Training Centre
National Police Training
Wyboston Lakes Leisure Centre
United Kingdom

Roland Lascola
Cyber Security Specialist
Independent Oversight
U.S. Department of Energy
Washington, D.C.

Barry Leese
Lieutenant
Maryland State Police
Computer Crimes Unit
Columbia, Maryland

Glenn Lewis
Kroll Global Headquarters
New York, New York

Jason Luttgens
Computer Specialist, R&D
NASA Office of the Inspector General
Computer Crimes Division
Washington, D.C.

Dan Mares
President
Mares and Company, LLC
Lawrenceville, Georgia

Ralph McNamara
Assistant Inspector General for
  Investigations
National Archives and Records
  Administration
Office of Inspector General
College Park, Maryland

Joel Moskowitz
Investigator
Clark County District Attorney's Office
Las Vegas, Nevada

James K. Pace
Senior Special Agent
Chief of Computer Forensics and
 Investigations
U.S. Army Criminal Investigation
 Laboratory
Forest Park, Georgia

Scott R. Patronik
Chief, Division of Technology and
 Advancement
Erie County Sheriff's Office
Buffalo, New York

Greg Redfern
Director
Department of Defense Computer
 Investigations Training Program
Linthicum, Maryland

Henry R. Reeve
General Counsel
Second Judicial District
Denver, Colorado

Jim Riccardi, Jr.
Electronic Crime Specialist
National Law Enforcement and Corrections
 Technology Center–Northeast
Rome, New York

Greg Schmidt
Investigations/Technical
Computer Forensics Examiner
Plano, Texas

Howard Schmidt
Vice Chair
President's Critical Infrastructure
 Protection Board
Washington, D.C.

Raemarie Schmidt
Computer Crimes Training Specialist
National White Collar Crime Center
Computer Crime Section
Fairmont, West Virginia

John A. Sgromolo
President
Digital Forensics, Inc.
Clearwater, Florida

George Sidor
Sr. Computer Forensics Investigator
G-Wag, Inc.
St. Albert, Alberta
Canada

Mike Weil
Computer Forensic Examiner
DoD Computer Forensics Laboratory
Linthicum, Maryland

Contents

Introduction

*Note: Terms that are defined in the glossary appear in **bold italics** on their first appearance in the body of the report.*

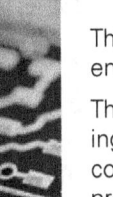

This guide is intended for use by law enforcement officers and other members of the law enforcement community who are responsible for the ***examination*** of ***digital evidence***.

This guide is not all-inclusive. Rather, it deals with common situations encountered during the examination of digital evidence. It is **not** a mandate for the law enforcement community; it is a guide agencies can use to help them develop their own policies and procedures.

Technology is advancing at such a rapid rate that the suggestions in this guide are best examined in the context of current technology and practices. Each case is unique and the judgment of the examiner should be given deference in the implementation of the procedures suggested in this guide. Circumstances of individual cases and Federal, State, and local laws/rules may also require actions other than those described in this guide.

When dealing with digital evidence, the following general forensic and procedural principles should be applied:

- Actions taken to secure and collect digital evidence should not affect the integrity of that evidence.

- Persons conducting an examination of digital evidence should be trained for that purpose.

- Activity relating to the seizure, examination, storage, or transfer of digital evidence should be documented, preserved, and available for review.

Through all of this, the examiner should be cognizant of the need to conduct an accurate and impartial examination of the digital evidence.

How is digital evidence processed?

Assessment. Computer forensic examiners should assess digital evidence thoroughly with respect to the scope of the case to determine the course of action to take.

Acquisition. Digital evidence, by its very nature, is fragile and can be altered, damaged, or destroyed by improper handling or examination. Examination is best conducted on a ***copy*** of the ***original evidence***. The original evidence should be acquired in a manner that protects and preserves the integrity of the evidence.

Examination. The purpose of the examination process is to extract and analyze digital evidence. Extraction refers to the recovery of data from its media. *Analysis* refers to the interpretation of the recovered data and putting it in a logical and useful format.

Documenting and reporting. Actions and observations should be documented throughout the forensic processing of evidence. This will conclude with the preparation of a written report of the findings.

Is your agency prepared to handle digital evidence?

This document recommends that agencies likely to handle digital evidence identify appropriate external resources for the processing of digital evidence before they are needed. These resources should be readily available for situations that are beyond the technical expertise or resources of the department. It is also recommended that agencies develop policies and procedures to ensure compliance with Federal, State, and local laws.

The following five topics describe the necessary basic steps to conduct a computer forensic examination and suggest the order in which they should be conducted. Although documentation is listed as the last step, a well-trained examiner understands that documentation is continuous throughout the entire examination process.

1. Policy and Procedure Development
2. Evidence Assessment
3. Evidence Acquisition
4. Evidence Examination
5. Documenting and Reporting

Each of these steps is explained further in the subsequent chapters. The chapters are further supported by the specialized information provided in the appendixes.

Chapter 1. Policy and Procedure Development

Principle: Computer forensics as a discipline demands specially trained personnel, support from management, and the necessary funding to keep a unit operating. This can be attained by constructing a comprehensive training program for examiners, sound digital evidence recovery techniques, and a commitment to keep any developed unit operating at maximum efficiency.

Procedure: Departments should create policies and procedures for the establishment and/or operation of a computer forensics unit.

Protocols and procedures

Mission statement

Developing policies and procedures that establish the parameters for operation and function is an important phase of creating a computer forensics unit. An effective way to begin this task is to develop a mission statement that incorporates the core functions of the unit, whether those functions include high-technology crime investigations, evidence collection, or forensic analysis.

Personnel

The policies and procedures should consider defining the personnel requirements for the unit. Topics that might be included in this section are job descriptions and minimum qualifications, hours of operation, on-call duty status, command structure, and team configuration.

Administrative considerations

Software licensing. Ensure that all software used by the computer forensics unit is properly licensed by the agency or an individual assigned to the unit.

Resource commitment. Establishing and operating a computer forensics unit may require *significant* allocation of financial resources and personnel. Many of the expenses are recurring and will have to be budgeted on a yearly basis. Resource allocation should include the type of facility that will house the unit, equipment used by examiners, software and hardware requirements, upgrades, training, and ongoing professional development and retention of examiners.

Training. It is important that computer forensics units maintain skilled, competent examiners. This can be accomplished by developing the skills of existing personnel or hiring individuals from specific disciplines. Because of the dynamic nature of the field, a comprehensive

ongoing training plan should be developed based on currently available training resources and should be considered in budget submissions. Consideration may also be given to mentor programs, on-the-job training, and other forms of career development.

Service request and intake

Guidelines should be developed to establish a process for the submission of forensic service requests and the intake of accepted requests for examination of digital evidence. Topics to consider in these guidelines include request and intake forms, point of contact, required documentation, acceptance criteria,* and requirements for the submission of physical evidence. Field personnel are expected to know the policies for service request and intake.

Case management

Once a request for forensic services is approved, criteria for prioritizing and assigning examinations should be determined and implemented. Criteria may include the nature of the crime, court dates, deadlines, potential victims, legal considerations, volatile nature of the evidence, and available resources.

Evidence handling and retention

Guidelines should be established for receiving, processing, documenting, and handling evidence and work products associated with the examination. The guidelines should be consistent with existing departmental policy. However, criteria for digital evidence handling and retention may exceed established departmental policies. **Note:** Evidence identified as contraband, such as child pornography, may require special consideration, such as obtaining specific contraband-related seizure and search warrants.

It is important to remember that other forensic disciplines might be able to recover other evidence, such as fingerprints on the hard drive, hair or fibers in the keyboard, and handwritten disk labels or printed material. In these instances, procedures should be developed to determine the order and manner in which examinations should be performed to reap full evidentiary value.

Case processing

Standard operating procedures (SOPs) should be developed for preserving and processing digital evidence. SOPs should be general enough to address the basic steps in a routine forensic examination while providing flexibility to respond to unique circumstances arising from unforeseen situations.

---

*One particular scenario for which an acceptance criteria policy and procedure may be helpful is one in which field personnel have made post-seizure changes to the evidence. This sometimes occurs when field personnel, often unaware of the effects of their actions, attempt to look for files on the original media, thereby changing date and time stamps associated with those files and possibly affecting other data on the media. Although perhaps not fatal to the case, this is one factor that likely would require documentation and should be considered before accepting this service request. One step in this procedure might be to submit the facts to the relevant prosecuting agency to determine whether it would consider the case to be viable, given the post-seizure alteration.

Developing technical procedures

Established procedures should guide the technical process of the examination of evidence. Procedures should be tested prior to their implementation to ensure that the results obtained are valid and independently reproducible. The steps in the development and validation of the procedures should be documented and include:

- Identifying the task or problem.

- Proposing possible solutions.

- Testing each solution on a known control sample.

- Evaluating the results of the test.

- Finalizing the procedure.

 Original evidence should never be used to develop procedures.

Chapter 2. Evidence Assessment

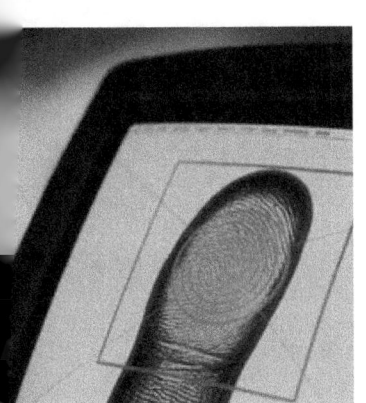

Principle: The digital evidence should be thoroughly assessed with respect to the scope of the case to determine the course of action.

Procedure: Conduct a thorough assessment by reviewing the search warrant or other legal authorization, case detail, nature of hardware and software, potential evidence sought, and the circumstances surrounding the *acquisition* of the evidence to be examined.

Case assessment

- Review the case investigator's request for service.

  — Identify the legal authority for the forensic examination request.

  — Ensure there is a completed request for assistance (see appendix D for examples).

  — Complete documentation of chain of custody.

- Consult with the case investigator about the case and let him or her know what the forensic examination may or may not discover. When talking with the investigator about the facts of the case, consider the following:

  — Discuss whether other forensic processes need to be performed on the evidence (e.g., DNA analysis, fingerprint, toolmarks, trace, and questioned documents).

  — Discuss the possibility of pursuing other investigative avenues to obtain additional digital evidence (e.g., sending a *preservation order* to an *Internet service provider (ISP)*, identifying remote storage locations, obtaining e-mail).

  — Consider the relevance of peripheral components to the investigation. For example, in forgery or fraud cases consider noncomputer equipment such as laminators, credit card blanks, check paper, scanners, and printers. In child pornography cases consider digital cameras.

  — Determine the potential evidence being sought (e.g., photographs, spreadsheets, documents, databases, financial records).

  — Determine additional information regarding the case (e.g., aliases, e-mail accounts, e-mail addresses, ISP used, names, *network* configuration and users, system logs, passwords, user names). This information may be obtained through interviews with the *system administrator*, users, and employees.

— Assess the skill levels of the computer users involved. Techniques employed by skilled users to conceal or destroy evidence may be more sophisticated (e.g., **encryption**, booby traps, **steganography**).

— Prioritize the order in which evidence is to be examined.

— Determine if additional personnel will be needed.

— Determine the equipment needed.

STOP The assessment might uncover evidence pertaining to other criminal activity (e.g., money laundering in conjunction with narcotics activities).

Onsite considerations

The following material does not provide complete information on examination of digital evidence; it is a general guide for law enforcement agencies that assess digital evidence at the crime scene. Readers may also want to consult *Electronic Crime Scene Investigation: A Guide for First Responders*, available at http://www.ojp.usdoj.gov/nij/pubs-sum/187736.htm.

STOP Consider safety of personnel at the scene. Always ensure the scene is properly secured before and during the search.

In some cases, the examiner may only have the opportunity to do the following while onsite:

■ Identify the number and type of computers.

■ Determine if a network is present.

■ Interview the system administrator and users.

■ Identify and document the types and volume of media, including **removable media**. Document the location from which the media was removed.

■ Identify offsite storage areas and/or remote computing locations.

■ Identify **proprietary software**.

- Evaluate general conditions of the site.

- Determine the operating system in question.

STOP Determine the need for and contact available outside resources, if necessary. Establish and retain a phone list of such resources.

Processing location assessment

Assess the evidence to determine where the examination should occur. It is preferable to complete an examination in a controlled environment, such as a dedicated forensic work area or laboratory. Whenever circumstances require an onsite examination to be conducted, attempt to control the environment. Assessment considerations might include the following:

- The time needed onsite to accomplish evidence recovery.

- Logistic and personnel concerns associated with long-term deployment.

- The impact on the business due to a lengthy search.

- The suitability of equipment, resources, media, training, and experience for an onsite examination.

Legal considerations

- Determine the extent of the authority to search.

- Identify possible concerns related to applicable Federal statutes (such as the Electronic Communications Privacy Act of 1986 (ECPA) and the Cable Communications Policy Act (CCPA), both as amended by the USA PATRIOT ACT of 2001, and/or the Privacy Protection Act of 1980 (PPA)), State statutes, and local policies and laws.

STOP If evidence is located that was not authorized in the original search authority, determine what additional legal process may be necessary to continue the search (e.g., warrant, amended consent form). Contact legal advisors for assistance if needed.

Evidence assessment

- Prioritize the evidence (e.g., distribution CDs versus user-created CDs).

  — Location where evidence is found.

  — Stability of media to be examined.

- Determine how to document the evidence (e.g., photograph, sketch, notes).

- Evaluate storage locations for ***electromagnetic interference***.

- Ascertain the condition of the evidence as a result of packaging, transport, or storage.

- Assess the need to provide continuous electric power to battery-operated devices.

Note: The procedures outlined are based on a compilation of generally accepted practices. Consult individual agency policy and seek legal advice, if necessary, before initiating an examination. Actual conditions may require alternative steps to those outlined in this guide. A thorough case assessment is a foundation for subsequent procedures.

Chapter 3. Evidence Acquisition

Principle: Digital evidence, by its very nature, is fragile and can be altered, damaged, or destroyed by improper handling or examination. For these reasons special precautions should be taken to preserve this type of evidence. Failure to do so may render it unusable or lead to an inaccurate conclusion.

Procedure: Acquire the original digital evidence in a manner that protects and preserves the evidence. The following bullets outline the basic steps:

- Secure digital evidence in accordance with departmental guidelines. In the absence of such guidelines, useful information can be found in *Electronic Crime Scene Investigation: A Guide for First Responders* (http://www.ojp.usdoj.gov/nij/pubs-sum/187736.htm).

- Document hardware and software configuration of the examiner's system.

- Verify operation of the examiner's computer system to include hardware and software.

- Disassemble the case of the computer to be examined to permit physical access to the storage devices.

  — Take care to ensure equipment is protected from static electricity and magnetic fields.

- Identify storage devices that need to be acquired. These devices can be internal, external, or both.

- Document internal storage devices and hardware configuration.

  — Drive condition (e.g., make, model, geometry, size, jumper settings, location, drive interface).

  — Internal components (e.g., sound card; video card; network card, including ***media access control (MAC)*** address; personal computer memory card international association (PCMCIA) cards).

- Disconnect storage devices (using the power connector or data cable from the back of the drive or from the motherboard) to prevent the destruction, damage, or alteration of data.

- Retrieve configuration information from the suspect's system through controlled boots.

  — Perform a controlled boot to capture **CMOS/BIOS** information and test functionality.

    ▪ Boot sequence (this may mean changing the BIOS to ensure the system boots from the floppy or CD-ROM drive).

    ▪ Time and date.

    ▪ Power on passwords.

  — Perform a second controlled boot to test the computer's functionality and the forensic boot disk.

    ▪ Ensure the power and data cables are properly connected to the floppy or CD-ROM drive, and ensure the power and data cables to the storage devices are still disconnected.

    ▪ Place the forensic boot disk into the floppy or CD-ROM drive. Boot the computer and ensure the computer will boot from the forensic boot disk.

  — Reconnect the storage devices and perform a third controlled boot to capture the drive configuration information from the CMOS/BIOS.

    ▪ Ensure there is a forensic boot disk in the floppy or CD-ROM drive to prevent the computer from accidentally booting from the storage devices.

    ▪ Drive configuration information includes logical block addressing (LBA); large disk; cylinders, heads, and sectors (CHS); or auto-detect.

- Power system down.

- Whenever possible, remove the subject storage device and perform the acquisition using the examiner's system. When attaching the subject device to the examiner's system, configure the storage device so that it will be recognized.

- Exceptional circumstances, including the following, may result in a decision not to remove the storage devices from the subject system:

  — RAID (redundant array of inexpensive disks). Removing the disks and acquiring them individually may not yield usable results.

  — Laptop systems. The system drive may be difficult to access or may be unusable when detached from the original system.

  — Hardware dependency (legacy equipment). Older drives may not be readable in newer systems.

  — Equipment availability. The examiner does not have access to necessary equipment.

— Network storage. It may be necessary to use the network equipment to acquire the data.

When using the subject computer to acquire digital evidence, reattach the subject storage device and attach the examiner's evidence storage device (e.g., hard drive, tape drive, **CD-RW**, **MO**).

- Ensure that the examiner's storage device is **forensically** clean when acquiring the evidence.

STOP **Write protection** should be initiated, if available, to preserve and protect original evidence.

Note: The examiner should consider creating a known value for the subject evidence prior to acquiring the evidence (e.g., performing an independent cyclic redundancy check (CRC), **hashing**). Depending on the selected acquisition method, this process may already be completed.

- If hardware write protection is used:

  — Install a write protection device.

  — Boot system with the examiner's controlled operating system.

- If software write protection is used:

  — Boot system with the examiner-controlled operating system.

  — Activate write protection.

- Investigate the geometry of any storage devices to ensure that all space is accounted for, including host-protected data areas (e.g., nonhost specific data such as the partition table matches the physical geometry of the drive).

- Capture the electronic serial number of the drive and other user-accessible, host-specific data.

- Acquire the subject evidence to the examiner's storage device using the appropriate software and hardware tools, such as:

  — Stand-alone duplication software.

  — Forensic analysis software suite.

  — Dedicated hardware devices.

- Verify successful acquisition by comparing known values of the original and the copy or by doing a sector-by-sector comparison of the original to the copy.

Chapter 4. Evidence Examination

Principle: General forensic principles apply when examining digital evidence. Different types of cases and media may require different methods of examination. Persons conducting an examination of digital evidence should be trained for this purpose.

Procedure: Conduct the examination on data that have been acquired using accepted forensic procedures. Whenever possible, the examination should not be conducted on original evidence.

This chapter discusses the extraction and the analysis of digital evidence. Extraction refers to the recovery of data from the media. Analysis refers to the interpretation of the recovered data and placement of it in a logical and useful format (e.g., how did it get there, where did it come from, and what does it mean?). The concepts offered are intended to assist the examiner in developing procedures and structuring the examination of the digital evidence. These concepts are not intended to be all-inclusive and recognize that not all of the following techniques may be used in a case. It is up to the discretion of the examiner to select the appropriate approach.

When conducting evidence examination, consider using the following steps:

Step 1. Preparation

Prepare working directory/directories on separate media to which evidentiary files and data can be recovered and/or extracted.

Step 2. Extraction

Discussed below are two different types of extraction, physical and logical. The physical extraction phase identifies and recovers data across the entire physical drive without regard to *file system*. The logical extraction phase identifies and recovers files and data based on the installed operating system(s), file system(s), and/or application(s).

Physical extraction

During this stage the extraction of the data from the drive occurs at the physical level regardless of file systems present on the drive. This may include the following methods: keyword searching, file carving, and extraction of the partition table and unused space on the physical drive.

- Performing a keyword search across the physical drive may be useful as it allows the examiner to extract data that may not be accounted for by the operating system and file system.

- File carving utilities processed across the physical drive may assist in recovering and extracting useable files and data that may not be accounted for by the operating system and file system.

- Examining the partition structure may identify the file systems present and determine if the entire physical size of the hard drive is accounted for.

Logical extraction

During this stage the extraction of the data from the drive is based on the file system(s) present on the drive and may include data from such areas as active files, **deleted files**, **file slack**, and unallocated file space. Steps may include:

- Extraction of the file system information to reveal characteristics such as directory structure, file attributes, file names, date and time stamps, file size, and file location.

- Data reduction to identify and eliminate known files through the comparison of calculated hash values to authenticated hash values.

- Extraction of files pertinent to the examination. Methods to accomplish this may be based on file name and extension, file header, file content, and location on the drive.

- Recovery of deleted files.

- Extraction of **password-protected**, encrypted, and compressed data.

- Extraction of file slack.

- Extraction of the **unallocated space**.

Step 3. Analysis of extracted data

Analysis is the process of interpreting the extracted data to determine their significance to the case. Some examples of analysis that may be performed include timeframe, data hiding, application and file, and ownership and possession. Analysis may require a review of the request for service, legal authority for the search of the digital evidence, investigative leads, and/or analytical leads.

Timeframe analysis

Timeframe analysis can be useful in determining when events occurred on a computer system, which can be used as a part of associating usage of the computer to an individual(s) at the time the events occurred. Two methods that can be used are:

- Reviewing the time and date stamps contained in the file system metadata (e.g., last modified, last accessed, created, change of status) to link files of interest to the timeframes relevant to the investigation. An example of this analysis would be using the last modified date and time to establish when the contents of a file were last changed.

- Reviewing system and application logs that may be present. These may include error logs, installation logs, connection logs, security logs, etc. For example, examination of a security log may indicate when a user name/password combination was used to log into a system.

Note: Take into consideration any differences in the individual's computer date and time as reported in the BIOS.

Data hiding analysis

Data can be concealed on a computer system. Data hiding analysis can be useful in detecting and recovering such data and may indicate knowledge, ownership, or intent. Methods that can be used include:

- Correlating the file headers to the corresponding file extensions to identify any mismatches. Presence of mismatches may indicate that the user intentionally hid data.

- Gaining access to all password-protected, encrypted, and **compressed files**, which may indicate an attempt to conceal the data from unauthorized users. A password itself may be as relevant as the contents of the file.

- Steganography.

- Gaining access to a **host-protected area (HPA)**. The presence of user-created data in an HPA may indicate an attempt to conceal data.

Application and file analysis

Many programs and files identified may contain information relevant to the investigation and provide insight into the capability of the system and the knowledge of the user. Results of this analysis may indicate additional steps that need to be taken in the extraction and analysis processes. Some examples include:

- Reviewing file names for relevance and patterns.

- Examining file content.

- Identifying the number and type of operating system(s).

- Correlating the files to the installed applications.

- Considering relationships between files. For example, correlating Internet history to cache files and e-mail files to e-mail attachments.

- Identifying unknown file types to determine their value to the investigation.

- Examining the users' default storage location(s) for applications and the **file structure** of the drive to determine if files have been stored in their default or an alternate location(s).

- Examining user-configuration settings.

- Analyzing file metadata, the content of the user-created file containing data additional to that presented to the user, typically viewed through the application that created it. For example, files created with word processing applications may include authorship, time last edited, number of times edited, and where they were printed or saved.

Ownership and possession

In some instances it may be essential to identify the individual(s) who created, modified, or accessed a file. It may also be important to determine ownership and knowledgeable possession of the questioned data. Elements of knowledgeable possession may be based on the analysis described above, including one or more of the following factors.

- Placing the subject at the computer at a particular date and time may help determine ownership and possession (timeframe analysis).

- Files of interest may be located in nondefault locations (e.g., user-created directory named "child porn") (application and file analysis).

- The file name itself may be of evidentiary value and also may indicate the contents of the file (application and file analysis).

- Hidden data may indicate a deliberate attempt to avoid detection (hidden data analysis).

- If the passwords needed to gain access to encrypted and password-protected files are recovered, the passwords themselves may indicate possession or ownership (hidden data analysis).

- Contents of a file may indicate ownership or possession by containing information specific to a user (application and file analysis).

Step 4. Conclusion

In and of themselves, results obtained from any one of these steps may not be sufficient to draw a conclusion. When viewed as a whole, however, associations between individual results may provide a more complete picture. As a final step in the examination process, be sure to consider the results of the extraction and analysis in their entirety.

Chapter 5. Documenting and Reporting

Principle: The examiner is responsible for completely and accurately reporting his or her findings and the results of the analysis of the digital evidence examination. Documentation is an ongoing process throughout the examination. It is important to accurately record the steps taken during the digital evidence examination.

Procedure: All documentation should be complete, accurate, and comprehensive. The resulting report should be written for the intended audience.

Examiner's notes

Documentation should be contemporaneous with the examination, and retention of notes should be consistent with departmental policies. The following is a list of general considerations that may assist the examiner throughout the documentation process.

- Take notes when consulting with the case investigator and/or prosecutor.

- Maintain a copy of the search authority with the case notes.

- Maintain the initial request for assistance with the case file.

- Maintain a copy of chain of custody documentation.

- Take notes detailed enough to allow complete duplication of actions.

- Include in the notes dates, times, and descriptions and results of actions taken.

- Document irregularities encountered and any actions taken regarding the irregularities during the examination.

- Include additional information, such as network topology, list of authorized users, user agreements, and/or passwords.

- Document changes made to the system or network by or at the direction of law enforcement or the examiner.

- Document the operating system and relevant software version and current, installed patches.

- Document information obtained at the scene regarding remote storage, remote user access, and offsite backups.

STOP During the course of an examination, information of evidentiary value may be found that is beyond the scope of the current legal authority. Document this information and bring it to the attention of the case agent because the information may be needed to obtain additional search authorities.

Examiner's report

This section provides guidance in preparing the report that will be submitted to the investigator, prosecutor, and others. These are general suggestions; departmental policy may dictate report writing specifics, such as its order and contents. The report may include:

- Identity of the reporting agency.

- Case identifier or submission number.

- Case investigator.

- Identity of the submitter.

- Date of receipt.

- Date of report.

- Descriptive list of items submitted for examination, including serial number, make, and model.

- Identity and signature of the examiner.

- Brief description of steps taken during examination, such as string searches, graphics image searches, and recovering erased files.

- Results/conclusions.

The following sections have been found to be useful in other report formats. See appendix A for sample reports.

Summary of findings

This section may consist of a brief summary of the results of the examinations performed on the items submitted for analysis. All findings listed in the summary should also be contained in the details of findings section of the report.

Details of findings

This section should describe in greater detail the results of the examinations and may include:

- Specific files related to the request.

- Other files, including deleted files, that support the findings.

- String searches, keyword searches, and text string searches.

- Internet-related evidence, such as Web site traffic analysis, chat logs, cache files, e-mail, and news group activity.

- Graphic image analysis.

- Indicators of ownership, which could include program registration data.

- Data analysis.

- Description of relevant programs on the examined items.

- Techniques used to hide or mask data, such as encryption, steganography, hidden attributes, hidden partitions, and *file name anomalies*.

Supporting materials

List supporting materials that are included with the report, such as printouts of particular items of evidence, digital copies of evidence, and chain of custody documentation.

Glossary

A glossary may be included with the report to assist the reader in understanding any technical terms used. Use a generally accepted source for the definition of the terms and include appropriate references.

Appendix A. Case Examples

The following two case briefs are examples of what could be involved in case analysis.

Disclaimer: The chosen case scenarios are for instructional purposes only and any association to an actual case and litigation is purely coincidental. Names and locations presented in the case scenarios are fictitious and are not intended to reflect actual people or places. Reference herein to any specific commercial products, processes, or services by trade name, trademark, manufacturer, or otherwise does not constitute or imply its endorsement, recommendation, or favoring by the U.S., State, or local governments, and the information and statements shall not be used for the purposes of advertising.

Case brief 1

SUBJECT owned a roofing company. SUBJECT gave his laptop computer to an employee to take to Mom & Pop's Computer Repair for monitor problems. Upon repairing the laptop, Mom of Mom & Pop's started the laptop to ensure the monitor had been fixed. A standard procedure of Mom & Pop's was to go to the *Recent* menu on the *Start Bar* of Windows® 98 systems and select files for viewing. Mom was presented with what appeared to be an image of a young child depicted in a sexually explicit manner. Mom telephoned the county sheriff. A sheriff's deputy responded and observed the image and confirmed it to be a violation of a State statute. The laptop was seized because it contained contraband. The seizure was performed in a manner consistent with recommendations found in *Electronic Crime Scene Investigation: A Guide for First Responders*. The laptop was entered into evidence according to agency policy, and a search warrant was obtained for the examination of the computer. The computer was submitted for examination.

Objective: To determine whether SUBJECT possessed child pornography. This was complicated by the number of people who handled the laptop.

Computer type: Generic laptop, serial # 123456789.

Operating system: Microsoft® Windows® 98.

Offense: Possession of child pornography.

Case agent: Investigator Johnson.

Evidence number: 012345.

Chain of custody: See attached form.

Where examination took place: Criminal investigations unit.

Tools used: Disk acquisition utility, universal graphic viewer, command line.

Processing

Assessment: Reviewed the case investigator's request for service. The search warrant provided legal authority. The investigator was interested in finding all information pertaining to child pornography, access dates, and ownership of the computer. It was determined that the equipment needed was available in the forensic lab.

Acquisition: The hardware configuration was documented and a ***duplicate*** of the hard drive was created in a manner that protected and preserved the evidence. The CMOS information, including the time and date, was documented.

Examination: The directory and file structures, including file dates and times, were recorded. A file header search was conducted to locate all graphic images. The image files were reviewed and those files containing images of what appeared to be children depicted in a sexually explicit manner were preserved. Shortcut files were recovered that pointed to files on floppy disks with sexually explicit file names involving children. The last accessed time and date of the files indicated the files were last accessed 10 days before the laptop was delivered to Mom & Pop's.

Documentation and reporting: The investigator was given a report describing the findings of the examination. The investigator determined that he needed to conduct interviews.

Next step: The employee who delivered the laptop computer to Mom & Pop's Computer Repair was interviewed, and he indicated that he had never operated the computer. Further, the employee stated SUBJECT had shown him images of a sexual nature involving children on the laptop. SUBJECT told the employee that he keeps his pictures on floppy disks at home; he just forgot this one image on the laptop.

The State's Attorney's Office was briefed in hope of obtaining a search warrant for SUBJECT's home based on the examination of the digital evidence and the interview of the employee. A warrant was drafted, presented to a judicial officer, and signed. During the subsequent search, floppy disks were discovered at SUBJECT's house. Forensic examination of the floppies revealed additional child pornography, including images in which SUBJECT was a participant. This resulted in the arrest of SUBJECT.

Case brief 1 report

REPORT OF MEDIA ANALYSIS

MEMORANDUM FOR: County Sheriff's Police
Investigator Johnson
Anytown, USA 01234

SUBJECT: Forensic Media Analysis Report
SUBJECT: DOE, JOHN
Case Number: 012345

1. Status: Closed.

2. Summary of Findings:

- 327 files containing images of what appeared to be children depicted in a sexually explicit manner were recovered.

- 34 shortcut files that pointed to files on floppy disks with sexually explicit file names involving children were recovered.

3. Items Analyzed:

TAG NUMBER:	ITEM DESCRIPTION:
012345	One Generic laptop, Serial # 123456789

4. Details of Findings:

- Findings in this paragraph related to the Generic Hard Drive, Model ABCDE, Serial # 3456ABCD, recovered from Tag Number 012345, One Generic laptop, Serial # 123456789.

  1) The examined hard drive was found to contain a Microsoft® Windows® 98 operating system.

  2) The directory and file listing for the media was saved to the Microsoft® Access Database TAG012345.MDB.

  3) The directory C:\JOHN DOE\PERSONAL\FAV PICS\, was found to contain 327 files containing images of what appeared to be children depicted in a sexually explicit manner. The file directory for 327 files disclosed that the files' creation date and times are 5 July 2001 between 11:33 p.m. and 11:45 p.m., and the last access date for 326 files listed is 27 December 2001. In addition, the file directory information for one file disclosed the last access date as 6 January 2002.

  4) The directory C:\JOHN DOE\PERSONAL\FAV PICS TO DISK\ contained 34 shortcut files that pointed to files on floppy disks with sexually explicit file names involving children. The file directory information for the 34 shortcut files disclosed

the files' creation date and times are 5 July 2001 between 11:23 p.m. and 11:57 p.m., and the last access date for the 34 shortcut files was listed as 5 July 2001.

5) The directory C:\JOHN DOE\LEGAL\ contained five Microsoft® Word documents related to various contract relationships John Doe Roofing had with other entities.

6) The directory C:\JOHN DOE\JOHN DOE ROOFING\ contained files related to operation of John Doe Roofing.

7) No further user-created files were present on the media.

5. Glossary:

Shortcut File: A file created that links to another file.

6. Items Provided: In addition to this hard copy report, one compact disk (CD) was submitted with an electronic copy of this report. The report on CD contains hyperlinks to the above-mentioned files and directories.

IMA D. EXAMINER   Released by_____
Computer Forensic Examiner

Case brief 2

A concerned citizen contacted the police department regarding possible stolen property. He told police that while he was searching the Internet, hoping to find a motorcycle for a reasonable price, he found an ad that met his requirements. This ad listed a Honda motorcycle for a low price, so he contacted the seller. Upon meeting the seller he became suspicious that the motorcycle was stolen. After hearing this information, police alerted the Auto Theft Unit. The Auto Theft Unit conducted a sting operation to purchase the motorcycle. Undercover officers met with the suspect, who, after receiving payment, provided them with the vehicle, a vehicle title, registration card, and insurance card. The suspect was arrested and the vehicle he was driving was searched incident to his arrest. During the search, a notebook computer was seized. Although the documents provided by the suspect looked authentic, document examiners determined that the documents were counterfeit. The auto theft investigator contacted the computer forensic laboratory for assistance in examining the seized computer. The investigator obtained a search warrant to analyze the computer and search for materials used in making counterfeit documents and other evidence related to the auto theft charges. The laptop computer was submitted to the computer forensic laboratory for analysis.

Objective: Determine if the suspect used the laptop computer as an instrument of the crimes of Auto Theft, Fraud, Forgery, Uttering False Documents, and Possession of Counterfeit Vehicle Titles and/or as a repository of data related to those crimes.

Computer type: Gateway Solo® 9100 notebook computer.

Operating system: Microsoft® Windows® 98.

Offenses: Auto Theft, Fraud, Forgery, Uttering False Documents, and Possession of Counterfeit Vehicle Titles.

Case agent: Auto Theft Unit Investigator.

Where examination took place: Computer Forensic Laboratory.

Tools used: Guidance Software™ EnCase®, DIGit©, Jasc Software™ Quick View Plus®, and AccessData™ Password Recovery Tool Kit™.

Processing

Assessment

1. Documentation provided by the investigator was reviewed.

   a. Legal authority was established by a search warrant obtained specifically for the examination of the computer in a laboratory setting.

   b. Chain of custody was properly documented on the appropriate departmental forms.

   c. The request for service and a detailed summary explained the investigation, provided keyword lists, and provided information about the suspect, the stolen vehicle, the counterfeit documents, and the Internet advertisement. The investigator also provided photocopies of the counterfeit documents.

2. The computer forensic investigator met with the case agent and discussed additional investigative avenues and potential evidence being sought in the investigation.

3. Evidence intake was completed.

   a. The evidence was marked and photographed.

   b. A file was created and the case information was entered into the laboratory database.

   c. The computer was stored in the laboratory's property room.

4. The case was assigned to a computer forensic investigator.

Imaging

1. The notebook computer was examined and photographed.

   a. The hardware was examined and documented.

   b. A controlled boot disk was placed in the computer's floppy drive. The computer was powered on and the BIOS setup program was entered. The BIOS information was documented and the system time was compared to a trusted time source and documented. The boot sequence was checked and documented; the system was already set to boot from the floppy drive first.

   c. The notebook computer was powered off without making any changes to the BIOS.

2. EnCase® was used to create an evidence file containing the **image** of the notebook computer's hard drive.

   a. The notebook computer was connected to a laboratory computer through a null-modem cable, which connected to the computers' parallel ports.

   b. The notebook computer was booted to the DOS prompt with a controlled boot disk and EnCase® was started in server mode.

   c. The laboratory computer, equipped with a magneto-optical drive for file storage, was booted to the DOS prompt with a controlled boot disk. EnCase® was started in server mode and evidence files for the notebook computer were acquired and written to magneto-optical disks.

   d. When the imaging process was completed, the computers were powered off.

      i. The notebook computer was returned to the laboratory property room.

      ii. The magneto-optical disks containing the EnCase® evidence files were write-protected and entered into evidence.

Analysis

1. A laboratory computer was prepared with Windows® 98, EnCase® for Windows, and other forensic software programs.

2. The EnCase® evidence files from the notebook computer were copied to the laboratory computer's hard drive.

3. A new EnCase® case file was opened and the notebook computer's evidence files were examined using EnCase®.

   a. Deleted files were recovered by EnCase®.

   b. File data, including file names, dates and times, physical and logical size, and complete path, were recorded.

   c. Keyword text searches were conducted based on information provided by the investigator. All hits were reviewed.

   d. Graphics files were opened and viewed.

   e. HTML files were opened and viewed.

   f. Data files were opened and viewed; two password-protected and encrypted files were located.

   g. Unallocated and slack space were searched.

   h. Files of evidentiary value or investigative interest were copied/unerased from the EnCase® evidence file and copied to a compact disk.

4. Unallocated clusters were copied/unerased from the EnCase® evidence file to a clean hard drive, wiped to U.S. Department of Defense recommendations (DoD 5200.28-STD). DIGit© was then used to carve images from unallocated space. The carved images were extracted from DIGit©, opened, and viewed. A total of 8,476 images were extracted.

5. The password-protected files were copied/unerased to a 1.44 MB floppy disk. AccessData™ Password Recovery Tool Kit™ was run on the files and passwords were recovered for both files. The files were opened using the passwords and viewed.

Findings

The analysis of the notebook computer resulted in the recovery of 176 files of evidentiary value or investigative interest. The recovered files included:

1. 59 document files including documents containing the suspect's name and personal information; text included in the counterfeit documents; scanned payroll, corporate, and certified checks; text concerning and describing stolen items; and text describing the recovered motorcycle.

2. 38 graphics files including high-resolution image files depicting payroll, corporate, and certified checks; U.S. currency; vehicle titles; registration cards and driver's license templates from Georgia and other States; insurance cards from various companies; and counterfeit certified checks payable to a computer company ranging from $25,000 to $40,000 for the purchase of notebook computers. Most graphics were scanned.

3. 63 HTML files including Hotmail® and Yahoo® e-mail and classified advertisements for the recovered motorcycle, other vehicles, and several brands of notebook computers; e-mail text, including e-mails between the suspect and the concerned citizen concerning the sale of the recovered motorcycle; and e-mails between the suspect and a computer company concerning the purchase of notebook computers.

4. 14 graphics files carved from unallocated space depicting checks at various stages of completion and scanned images of U.S. currency.

5. Two password-protected and encrypted files.

   a. WordPerfect® document containing a list of personal information on several individuals including names, addresses, dates of birth, credit card and bank account numbers and expiration dates, checking account information, and other information. Password [**nomoresecrets**].

   b. Microsoft® Word document containing vehicle title information for the recovered motorcycle. Password [**HELLO**].

Documentation

1. Forensic Report – All actions, processes, and findings were described in a detailed Forensic Report, which is maintained in the laboratory case file.

2. Police Report – The case agent was provided with a police report describing the evidence examined, techniques used, and the findings.

3. Work Product – A compact disk containing files and file data of evidentiary value or investigative interest was created. The original was stored in the laboratory case file. Copies were provided to the case agent and the prosecutor.

Summary

Based on the information revealed by the computer analysis, several new avenues of investigation were opened.

✔ By contacting the victims listed in the password-protected WordPerfect® document, investigators learned that the victims had all been robbed in the same city during the previous summer by an individual meeting the description of the suspect.

✔ Contact with the computer company revealed the counterfeit checks found on the suspect's computer had been accepted for the purchase of computers, and that the computers were shipped to him and were the subject of an ongoing investigation. Model numbers and serial numbers provided by the computer company matched several of the Hotmail® and Yahoo® classified ads found on the suspect's computer.

✔ Several of the counterfeit checks found on the suspect's computer were already the subject of ongoing investigations.

✔ Information recovered concerning other vehicles led to the recovery of additional stolen vehicles.

✔ The specific information sought in the search warrant concerning the sale of the stolen motorcycle and the counterfeit documents was recovered from the suspect's computer.

Conclusion

The suspect eventually plead guilty and is now incarcerated.

Case brief 2 report

Department of State Police
Computer Crimes Unit
Computer Forensics Laboratory
7155-C Columbia Gateway Drive
Columbia, MD 21046
(410) 290-0000

April 19, 1999

MEMO TO FILE

FORENSIC EXAMINER PROCESSING NOTES:	**SGT. David B. Smith (5555)**
FORENSIC CASE NUMBER:	**99-03-333-A**

REQUESTER:	TFC. Brian Jones
	State Police Auto Theft Unit (310-288-8433)
OFFENSE:	Auto Theft, Forgery
CASE NUMBER:	01-39-00333
RECEIVED:	March 19, 1999
OPENED:	March 24, 1999
COMPLETED:	April 19, 1999
FORENSIC HOURS:	40 hours
OS EXAMINED:	Microsoft® Windows® 98
FILE SYSTEM:	[FAT32]
DATA ANALYZED:	7,782 MB

Evidence Description: Item 1: One Gateway Solo® 9100 Notebook Computer, Serial Number 555-Z3025-00-002-0433.

Action Taken:

March 24, 1999

1600 hours: I retrieved the original digital evidence from the CCU Property Room. I inventoried, marked, and cataloged the evidence described on the MSP Form 67. All original evidence listed on the Chain of Custody Form was accounted for.

1620 hours: I examined the Gateway Solo® 9100 notebook computer and completed an **Initial Computer Evidence Processing** form (see attached). The computer contained one fixed disk. The notebook case was not opened to expose the drive (Original Digital Evidence# hdd01). I inserted a controlled boot disk in the notebook computer floppy drive and powered on the computer. I pressed F1 to enter the setup utility. I documented the BIOS settings:

State Police - Computer Forensics Laboratory
Forensic Report - Laboratory Case Number 99-03-333-A

BIOS	System Date	System Time	Memory	Boot Order
Award 4.5 pg	3/24/1999	16:30:03	128 MB	Floppy Drive Hard Drive
	Actual Date 3/24/1999	Actual Time 16:30:08	CPU Intel PII 300	

EnCase® (1.998) (DOS Version 7.10)

1 Physical Disks					1 Logical Volumes				
Disk 0	Size 7.6GB		CHS 7480:16:63		LP	LABEL	SYSTEM	FREE	SIZE
Lock	Code	Type	Sectors	Size	C0	NONAME	FAT32	5.5GB	7.6GB
80	0B	FAT32	16,000,740	7.6GB					

Server Mode

Connected...!

En.exe was executed on the laboratory computer; EnCase® reported:

EnCase® (1.998) Client Mode (DOS Version 7.10)

1 Physical Disks					1 Logical Volumes				
Disk 0	Size 7.6GB		CHS 7480:16:63		LP	LABEL	SYSTEM	FREE	SIZE
Lock	Code	Type	Sectors	Size	C0	NONAME	FAT32	5.5GB	7.6GB
80	0B	FAT32	16,000,740	7.6GB					

State Police - Computer Forensics Laboratory
Forensic Report - Laboratory Case Number 99-03-333-A
3 of 6   Initials **DBS**

1750 hours: Acquisition of a compressed evidence file was started.

File Name & Path:	F:\hdd01
Case #:	01-39-00333
Examiner:	Sgt. David B. Smith
Evidence #:	99-03-333-A
Description:	555-Z3025-00-002-0433.

March 25, 1999

0900 hours: EnCase® reported: "An evidence file for drive 0 was successfully created . . . Elapsed Time 11:14:00, 7.6GB read, 0 errors, 11:14:00 elapsed, 0:00:00 remaining."

0910 hours: I exited EnCase® on the laboratory computer and returned to the A:\ prompt. The computer was powered off, the Sony MO disk containing the evidence files was removed from the MO drive unit and write protected and placed into evidence. A State Police Chain of Custody Form was completed.

March 30, 1999

1400 hours: The laboratory Gateway GX-450XL computer was equipped with a Sony MO drive unit connected to an AHA 2940UW SCSI adapter card. A controlled boot disk was placed in drive A:. The computer was powered on and the system booted to the A:\ prompt. The DOS copy command was used to copy the EnCase® evidence files from the Sony MO Dsk drive F: to "Data" hard drive, E:. The files were successfully copied. The computer was powered down and the Sony MO disk was returned to evidence.

April 1, 1999

0800 hours: The laboratory Gateway GX-450XL computer was booted to Windows® 98. EnCase® for Windows® 98 (version 1.999) was launched. I opened a new EnCase® case, titled *99-03-333-A*. I added the previously acquired evidence file into the case. EnCase® file Signatures was run.

0900 hours: I began a logical analysis of the data contained in the EnCase® case.

1000 hours: A data wiping utility was used to wipe removable drive I: on the laboratory Gateway GX-450XL computer. The drive was wiped to U.S. Department of Defense recommendations (DoD 5200.28-STD). Unallocated clusters and file slack from the evidence file space were then copied from the EnCase® case to drive I:. The files were divided into seven folders, each folder holding a maximum of 1,048MB. 575 files containing 5,944MB were copied.

State Police - Computer Forensics Laboratory
Forensic Report - Laboratory Case Number 99-03-333-A
4 of 6

Initials **DBS**

1220 hours: NCIS DIGit© [Version 1.08] was executed. The files that had been copied from the evidence file to drive I: were examined. The files included both unallocated clusters and file slack. 5,944MB of data were processed in seven (7) batches. DIGit© reported extracting:

Files Extracted From Unallocated Space
DIGit© (Version 1.08)

Batch	HITS	Jpg	Bmp	Gif	Tif	Pcx	HTML	Word8	Total Megs Examined
1	5,378	197	82	4,908	11	16	66	98	1,048
2	2,499	53	48	2,258	14	3	76	47	1,048
3	599	0	6	550	4	6	11	22	1,048
4	0	0	0	0	0	0	0	0	1,048
5	0	0	0	0	0	0	0	0	1,048
6	0	0	0	0	0	0	0	0	704
7	0	0	0	0	0	0	0	0	512 bytes
Total	8,476	250	136	7,716	29	25	153	167	5,944MB

The extracted graphic files were viewed using Quick View Plus®.

April 4, 1999

0930 hours: I continued the examination of the graphics and HTML files previously extracted from unallocated clusters using DIGit©.

1000 hours: I used EnCase® version 1.999 to perform a keyword text string search of the entire case. All hits were examined and text with possible evidentiary value was extracted.

> **Search 1:** **Keyword:** <u>honda</u> **Hits:** <u>433</u>

April 5, 1999

0700 hours: I continued the examination of HTML files previously extracted from unallocated clusters using DIGit©.

1354 hours I used EnCase® version 1.999 to perform a keyword text string search of the entire case. All hits were examined and text with possible evidentiary value was extracted.

> **Search 2:** **Keywords:** **99985** (case) **Hits: 0**
> **999886** (case) **1**
> **ZDF-3333** (case) **0**
> **39347618** **0**
> **virginia** **212**
> **georgia** **333**
> **certificate of title** **0**
>
> **Search 3:** **Keyword:** **motorcycle** **Hits: 1,696**

State Police - Computer Forensics Laboratory
Forensic Report - Laboratory Case Number 99-03-333-A
5 of 6   Initials **DBS**

April 6, 1999

0800 hours: I used EnCase® version 1.999 to perform a keyword text string search of the entire case. All hits were examined and text with possible evidentiary value was extracted.

Search 4:	**Keywords:**	**suzuki gsxr**	**Hits:**	**2**
Search 5:	**Keyword:**	**brandell**	**Hits:**	**125**
Search 6:	**Keywords:**	**jh2sc3307wm20333**	**Hits:**	**5**
		..#..####..######(Grep)		**0**
Search 7:	**Keyword:**	**Jn8hd17y5nw011333**	**Hits:**	**0**

April 7, 1999

0800 hours: I continued the examination of the search results.

1333 hours: I used EnCase® version 1.999 to perform a keyword text string search of the entire case. All hits were examined and text with possible evidentiary value was extracted.

Search 8:	**Keywords:**	**9998##(Grep)**	**Hits:**	**5**
		hotmail		**19,465**
		chyma		**27,453**
		suzuki		**20**

April 19, 1999

0700 hours: I continued the file-by-file examination of the evidence files.

0900 hours: I completed the forensic examination. Documents, pictures, HTML files, and text fragments of investigative interest were located by utilizing individual file-by-file examination, EnCase® Keyword Text Searches, and NCIS DIGit©. The Keyword Text Searches are defined in the EnCase® Report. Files believed to be of investigative interest were bookmarked into categories as defined below. The files associated with the information described below were copied/unerased from the EnCase® case.

FINDINGS

The analysis of the notebook computer resulted in the recovery of 176 files of evidentiary value or investigative interest. The recovered files included:

1. 59 document files including documents containing the suspect's name and personal information; text included in the counterfeit documents; scanned payroll, corporate, and certified checks; text concerning and describing stolen items; and text describing the recovered motorcycle.

2. 38 graphics files including high-resolution image files depicting payroll, corporate, and certified checks; U.S. currency; vehicle titles; registration cards and driver's license templates from Georgia and other States; insurance cards from various

State Police - Computer Forensics Laboratory
Forensic Report - Laboratory Case Number 99-03-333-A
6 of 6   Initials **DBS**

companies; and counterfeit certified checks payable to a computer company ranging from $25,000 to $40,000 for the purchase of notebook computers. Most graphics were scanned.

3. 63 HTML files including Hotmail® and Yahoo® e-mail and classified advertisements for the recovered motorcycle, other vehicles, and several brands of notebook computers; e-mail text, including e-mails between the suspect and the concerned citizen about the sale of the recovered motorcycle; e-mails between the suspect and a computer company concerning the purchase of notebook computers.

4. 14 graphics files carved from unallocated space depicting checks at various stages of completion and scanned images of U.S. currency.

5. Two password-protected and encrypted files.

   a. WordPerfect® document containing a list of personal information on several individuals including names, addresses, dates of birth, credit card and bank account numbers and expiration dates, checking account information, and other information. Password [**nomoresecrets**].

   b. Microsoft® Word document containing vehicle title information for the recovered motorcycle. Password [**HELLO**].

I created one compact disk containing copies of the above-described files, which will be maintained in the CFL case file. A copy of the compact disk was labeled and provided to the investigator.

1800 hours: The forensic examination was completed.

Sgt. David B. Smith (5555) [Signature]

Appendix B. Glossary

The following terms are included to assist the reader in understanding this guide.

Acquisition: A process by which digital evidence is duplicated, copied, or imaged.

Analysis: To look at the results of an examination for its significance and probative value to the case.

BIOS: Basic Input Output System. The set of routines stored in read-only memory that enables a computer to start the operating system and to communicate with the various devices in the system such as disk drives, keyboard, monitor, printer, and communication ports.

CD-RW: Compact disk-rewritable. A disk to which data can be written and erased.

CMOS: Complementary metal oxide semiconductor. A type of chip used to store BIOS configuration information.

Compressed file: A file that has been reduced in size through a compression algorithm to save disk space. The act of compressing a file will make it unreadable to most programs until the file is uncompressed. Most common compression utilities are PKZIP with an extension of .zip.

Copy: An accurate reproduction of information contained on an original physical item, independent of the electronic storage device (e.g., logical file copy). Maintains contents, but attributes may change during the reproduction.

Deleted files: If a subject knows there are incriminating files on the computer, he or she may delete them in an effort to eliminate the evidence. Many computer users think that this actually eliminates the information. However, depending on how the files are deleted, in many instances a forensic examiner is able to recover all or part of the original data.

Digital evidence: Information stored or transmitted in binary form that may be relied on in court.

Duplicate: An accurate digital reproduction of all data contained on a digital storage device (e.g., hard drive, CD-ROM, flash memory, floppy disk, Zip®, Jaz®). Maintains contents and attributes (e.g., bit stream, bit copy, and sector dump).

Electromagnetic interference: An electromagnetic disturbance that interrupts, obstructs, or otherwise degrades or limits the effective performance of electronics/electrical equipment.

Encryption: Any procedure used in cryptography to convert plain text into cipher text in order to prevent anyone but the intended recipient from reading that data.

Examination: Technical review that makes the evidence visible and suitable for analysis; tests performed on the evidence to determine the presence or absence of specific data.

File name anomaly: Header/extension mismatch; file name inconsistent with the content of the file.

File slack: Space between the logical end of the file and the end of the last allocation unit for that file.

File structure: How an application program stores the contents of a file.

File system: The way the operating system keeps track of the files on the drive.

Forensically clean: Digital media that are completely wiped of nonessential and residual data, scanned for viruses, and verified before use.

Hashing: The process of using a mathematical algorithm against data to produce a numeric value that is representative of that data.

Host protected area: An area that can be defined on *IDE* drives that meets the technical specifications as defined by ATA4 and later. If a Max Address has been set that is less than a Native Max Address, then a host protected area is present.

IDE: Integrated drive electronics. A type of data communications interface generally associated with storage devices.

Image: An accurate digital representation of all data contained on a digital storage device (e.g., hard drive, CD-ROM, flash memory, floppy disk, Zip®, Jaz®). Maintains contents and attributes, but may include metadata such as CRCs, hash value, and audit information.

ISP: Internet service provider. An organization that provides access to the Internet. Small Internet service providers provide service via modem and an integrated services digital network (ISDN), while the larger ones also offer private line hookups (e.g., T1, fractional T1).

MAC address: Media access control address. A unique identifying number built (or "burned") into a network interface card by the manufacturer.

MO: Magneto-optical. A drive used to back up files on a personal computer using magnetic and optical technologies.

Network: A group of computers connected to one another to share information and resources.

Original evidence: Physical items and the data objects that are associated with those items at the time of seizure.

Password protected: Many software programs include the ability to protect a file using a password. One type of password protection is sometimes called "access denial." If this feature is used, the data will be present on the disk in the normal manner, but the software program will not open or display the file without the user entering the password. In many cases, forensic examiners are able to bypass this feature.

Preservation Order: A document ordering a person or company to preserve potential evidence. The authority for preservation letters to ISPs is in 18 USC 2703(f).

Proprietary software: Software that is owned by an individual or company and that requires the purchase of a license.

Removable media: Items (e.g., floppy disks, CDs, DVDs, cartridges, tape) that store data and can be easily removed.

SCSI: Small Computer System Interface. A type of data communications interface.

Steganography: The art and science of communicating in a way that hides the existence of the communication. It is used to hide a file inside another. For example, a child pornography image can be hidden inside another graphic image file, audio file, or other file format.

System administrator: The individual who has legitimate supervisory rights over a computer system. The administrator maintains the highest access to the system. Also can be known as sysop, sysadmin, and system operator.

Unallocated space: Allocation units not assigned to active files within a file system.

Write protection: Hardware or software methods of preventing data from being written to a disk or other medium.

Appendix C. Sample Worksheets

These worksheets are specific to the Drug Enforcement Administration and are provided as examples.

Computer Evidence Worksheet

Case Number: _____ **Exhibit Number:** _____

Laboratory Number: _____ **Control Number:** _____

Computer Information

Manufacturer: _____ Model: _____
Serial Number: _____
Examiner Markings: _____
Computer Type: Desktop ☐ Laptop ☐ Other: _____
Computer Condition: Good ☐ Damaged ☐ **(See Remarks)**
Number of Hard Drives: _____ 3.5" Floppy Drive ☐ 5.25" Floppy Drive ☐
Modem ☐ Network Card ☐ Tape Drive ☐ Tape Drive Type: _____
100 MB Zip ☐ 250 MB Zip ☐ CD Reader ☐ CD Read/Write ☐
DVD ☐ Other: _____

CMOS Information	Not Available ☐
Password Logon: Yes ☐ No ☐ Password = _____	
Current Time: _____ AM ☐ PM ☐ Current Date: _____ / _____ / _____	
CMOS Time: _____ AM ☐ PM ☐ CMOS Date: _____ / _____ / _____	

CMOS Hard Drive #1 Settings	Auto ☐
Capacity: _____ Cylinders: _____ Heads: _____ Sectors: _____	
Mode: LBA ☐ Normal ☐ Auto ☐ Legacy CHS ☐	

CMOS Hard Drive #2 Settings	Auto ☐
Capacity: _____ Cylinders: _____ Heads: _____ Sectors: _____	
Mode: LBA ☐ Normal ☐ Auto ☐ Legacy CHS ☐	

Computer Evidence Worksheet	**Page 1 of 2**

Sub Exhibits Split From This Computer

Sub Number	Type	Where Found

Remarks

Computer Evidence Worksheet	Page 2 of 2

Hard Drive Evidence Worksheet

Case Number: _____   **Exhibit Number:** _____

Laboratory Number: _____   **Control Number:** _____

<u>**Hard Drive #1 Label Information**</u> [**Not Available** ☐]   <u>**Hard Drive #2 Label Information**</u> [**Not Available** ☐]

Manufacturer: _____	Manufacturer: _____
Model: _____	Model: _____
Serial Number: _____	Serial Number: _____
Capacity: _____ Cylinders: _____	Capacity: _____ Cylinders: _____
Heads: _____ Sectors: _____	Heads: _____ Sectors: _____
Controller Rev. _____	Controller Rev. _____
IDE ☐ 50 Pin SCSI ☐	IDE ☐ 50 Pin SCSI ☐
68 Pin SCSI ☐ 80 Pin SCSI ☐ Other ☐	68 Pin SCSI ☐ 80 Pin SCSI ☐ Other ☐
Jumper: Master ☐ Slave ☐	Jumper: Master ☐ Slave ☐
Cable Select ☐ Undetermined ☐	Cable Select ☐ Undetermined ☐

Hard Drive #1 Parameter Information

DOS FDisk ☐   PTable ☐   PartInfo ☐   Linux FDisk ☐   SafeBack ☐   EnCase ☐   Other:

Capacity: _____   Cylinders: _____   Heads: _____   Sectors: _____

LBA Addressable Sectors: _____   Formatted Drive Capacity: _____

Volume Label: _____

Partitions

Name:	Bootable?	Start:	End:	Type:
_____	☐	_____	_____	_____
_____	☐	_____	_____	_____
_____	☐	_____	_____	_____
	☐			

Hard Drive #2 Parameter Information

DOS FDisk ☐   PTable ☐   PartInfo ☐   Linux FDisk ☐   SafeBack ☐   EnCase ☐   Other:

Capacity: _____   Cylinders: _____   Heads: _____   Sectors: _____

LBA Addressable Sectors: _____   Formatted Drive Capacity: _____

Volume Label: _____

Partitions

Name:	Bootable?	Start:	End:	Type:
_____	☐	_____	_____	_____
_____	☐	_____	_____	_____
_____	☐	_____	_____	_____
	☐			

Hard Drive Evidence Worksheet	**Page 1 of 2**

Image Archive Information

Archive Method: Direct to Tape ☐ NTBackup ☐ Tar ☐ Other :* _____ Compressed? ☐	
Attach appropriate worksheet for backup method used.	
Tape Type: DAT 24 ☐ Dat 40 ☐ DLT ☐* Other *: _____ Number Used:	

*Requires Lab Director Approval

Analysis Platform Information

Operating Systems Used: DOS ☐ Windows ☐ Mac ☐ *nix ☐ Other: _____

Version: _____

Analysis Software Base: I-Look ☐ EnCase ☐ DOS Utilities ☐ *nix Utilities ☐ Other:*

Version: _____

Restored Work Copy/Image Validated: Yes ☐ No ☐

List of utilities used other than base

Utility	Version	Purpose

Analysis Milestones

Milestone	Remarks	Initials
Run Anti-Virus Scan		
Full File List with Meta Data		
Identify Users/Logons/ISP Accounts, etc.		
Browse File System		
Keyword/String Search		
Web/E-mail Header Recovery		
Recover & Examine Free/Slack Space		
Examine Swap		
Unerase/Recover Deleted Files		
Execute Programs as Needed		
Examine/Recover Mail/Chat		
Crack Passwords		

Hard Drive Evidence Worksheet	**Page 2 of 2**

Removable Media Worksheet

Case Number: _____   **Exhibit Number:** _____

Laboratory Number: _____   **Control Number:** _____

Media Type / Quantity

Diskette [ ]	LS-120 [ ]	100 MB Zip [ ]	250 MB Zip [ ]
1 GB Jaz [ ]	2 GB Jaz [ ]	Magneto-Optical [ ]	Tape [ ]
CD [ ]	DVD [ ]	Other [ ]	

Examination

Exhibit # Sub-Exhibit #	Triage	Duplicated	Browse	Unerase	Keyword Search
	☐	☐	☐	☐	☐
	☐	☐	☐	☐	☐
	☐	☐	☐	☐	☐
	☐	☐	☐	☐	☐
	☐	☐	☐	☐	☐
	☐	☐	☐	☐	☐
	☐	☐	☐	☐	☐
	☐	☐	☐	☐	☐
	☐	☐	☐	☐	☐
	☐	☐	☐	☐	☐
	☐	☐	☐	☐	☐
	☐	☐	☐	☐	☐
	☐	☐	☐	☐	☐
	☐	☐	☐	☐	☐
	☐	☐	☐	☐	☐
	☐	☐	☐	☐	☐
	☐	☐	☐	☐	☐

_____   _____   _____   _____
Examiner   **Date**   Supervisor Review   Date

Digital Evidence Removable Media Worksheet   **Page 1 of 2**

Exhibit # Sub-Exhibit #	Triage	Duplicated	Browse	Unerase	Keyword Search
	☐	☐	☐	☐	☐
	☐	☐	☐	☐	☐
	☐	☐	☐	☐	☐
	☐	☐	☐	☐	☐
	☐	☐	☐	☐	☐
	☐	☐	☐	☐	☐
	☐	☐	☐	☐	☐
	☐	☐	☐	☐	☐
	☐	☐	☐	☐	☐
	☐	☐	☐	☐	☐
	☐	☐	☐	☐	☐
	☐	☐	☐	☐	☐
	☐	☐	☐	☐	☐
	☐	☐	☐	☐	☐
	☐	☐	☐	☐	☐
	☐	☐	☐	☐	☐
	☐	☐	☐	☐	☐
	☐	☐	☐	☐	☐
	☐	☐	☐	☐	☐
	☐	☐	☐	☐	☐
	☐	☐	☐	☐	☐
	☐	☐	☐	☐	☐
	☐	☐	☐	☐	☐
	☐	☐	☐	☐	☐
	☐	☐	☐	☐	☐
	☐	☐	☐	☐	☐
	☐	☐	☐	☐	☐
	☐	☐	☐	☐	☐
	☐	☐	☐	☐	☐
	☐	☐	☐	☐	☐
	☐	☐	☐	☐	☐
	☐	☐	☐	☐	☐
	☐	☐	☐	☐	☐

Digital Evidence Removable Media Worksheet   **Page 2 of 2**

Appendix D. Examples of Request for Service Forms

Example 1: Regional Computer Forensics Lab •
4455 Genesee Street, Cheektowaga, NY 14225

REQUEST FOR SERVICE

CASE INFORMATION:				*RCFL Case #:*
Submitting Person/ID#:		Date:		Agency Case #:
Submitting Agency:		Service: **Field Lab Tech**		Case Title:
Agency Property Tag #:		Suspect's Name:		
Case Agent:		Phone #:		
DDA/AUSA Assigned:		Phone #:		
Date Seized:		Case/Crime Type:		
Location Seized:		Pending Court Dates:		
Site #:		Date Analysis Needed:		
Suspect In Custody:	**Yes/No**	Expected Evidence Return Date:		
Narcotics Related:	**Yes/No**	Number of Computers Anticipated:		
Type of Seizure: (Circle) **Search Warrant Probation Parole Consent Admin Fed. Grand Jury Other:**				
Has this evidence been previously viewed and/or accessed by anyone? (Explain)				
Are you aware of any privileged information contained within evidence? (Explain)				
Do you want Standard Case Related Search Strings run against evidence? **Yes/No** (Circle Requested Searches) **Child Porn Narcotics Financial Crimes Internet Crimes Extortion Other:**				

SERVICE REQUESTED: *(Requests for Field Service must be received at least 2 business days prior to the search.)*

_____

_____

_____

INSTRUCTIONS:

a. Please prepare one form for each search site (address).
b. Please provide **ALL** requested information and note any unusual circumstances in the Service Request area.
c. Please attach an Evidence Custody Form listing each individual container or package of submitted evidence.

RCFL USE ONLY **Date Case**	**Received By:**
Case Priority:	**Priority Established By:**

Example 2: DoD Computer Forensics Laboratory (DCFL) Intake Form

(Form has been edited)

DEPARTMENT OF THE AIR FORCE

AIR FORCE OFFICE OF SPECIAL INVESTIGATIONS

(USE YOUR OWN LETTER HEAD)

MEMORANDUM FOR RECORD DoD Computer Forensics Laboratory
12 June 2000

TO: DoD Computer Forensics Laboratory (DCFL)
911 Elkridge Landing Road, Suite 300
Linthicum, MD 21090

FROM: Self-Explanatory

SUBJECT: Request Forensic Media Analysis (Complete Unit Investigation Number)

NOTE: Do not remove the captions (the bold face lettering only. Please remove the explanations.). If no information can be applied to a certain caption, then state N/A or unknown.

1. ***FULL NAME OF SUBJECT: (If unknown, then state "Unknown.")

　　　　JOHN JIM DOE

2. ***PRIORITY: Explain if there is publicity, high-level interest, or other reasons to justify placing this investigation ahead of others (e.g., court date, etc.).

3. CLASSIFICATION: Unclassified–Secret–Specialized Compartmented Information, as it pertains to the investigation, and properly mark all documents.

4. ***CASE AGENT: (This is the "Lead" investigator. For example, if this is a joint investigation, then provide the identification of the "Lead Investigator" of the "Lead Investigating Agency." Provide complete identification and where they are located.) SA Max Factor, AFOSI Detachment 998, Home AFB, WV, DSN: 234–2345 or Commercial: (234) 234–2345.

NOTE: The DCFL does not have DSN service yet. Please provide commercial telephone numbers.

5. ***SYNOPSIS OF THE CASE FACTS: (Brief description of allegation, situation, and background surrounding the investigation. Provide information that will be useful to the

examiner so they can better understand the investigation and provide a better examination). You can provide an already completed document or a pending report to cover this step.

6. ***ITEMS TO BE ANALYZED: (NOTE: IF NOT EVIDENCE, STATE THAT FACT)

NOTE: It is only required to list the items to be analyzed, not to answer all the questions.

This must be a complete list of all items that need analysis. An evidence listing must completely identify all items. The following is just a sample of how to list evidence:

<u>Tag #'s</u>	<u>Description</u>
Tag # XX	Western Digital Caviar 31600 Hard Drive, Serial #: WT2891586134 taken from AST Computer Serial # 186AUZ022348.
Tag # XX	Fujitsu M1636TAU Hard Drive, Serial #: 08613105, Size: 1226MB.
Tag # XX	Gateway 2000, 386/33 MHz, Serial #: 302557386-330XC. Computer System with a Western Digital 125 MB internal hard drive, a Seagate 107 MB internal hard drive, internal 3.5-inch high-density floppy drive, one internal 5.25-inch floppy drive, internal sound card. Gateway 2000 101 Keyboard, Serial #: 9208572226f7. Computer Mouse Device, Serial #: 850753.
Tag # XX	198 each 3.5-inch floppy diskettes 1 each 5.25-inch floppy diskettes

7. ***SUPPORT REQUESTED: (Specific and detailed request. Do not just cut and paste what is listed below. These are just some sample statements. If you do not know what one of these items is, then don't include it. Also, don't just say "give me everything" and expect DCFL to take it from there. List items you need the DCFL to find and how you need it produced and provided to you.)

e.g. **Computer Media**

Extract all system logs, graphic files, text, documents, etc.
Examine file system for modification to operating system software or configuration.
Examine file system for back doors, check for setuid and setgid files.
Examine file system for any sign of a sniffer program.
Extract data from this 8-mm tape and convert to readable format, cut to CD.
Backup hard drives and place backup on a CD, tape, or other format.
Analyze for deleted files and restore deleted files, cut findings to CD.
If possible, correlate sexually explicit images to the Internet history file.
Extract sexually explicit images from logical, slack space, free space, cut to CD.
Extract all pertinent text files of a sexual nature.
Provide an analysis report and cut all findings to CD (specify).
Conduct string search on physical level of media (provide list of words).

8. PERTINENT DATA: (e.g., provide passwords, keyword lists, operating system, nicknames, computer types, network information, Internet Protocol Address, and any other information that will assist with the analysis.)

NOTE: If network intrusion detection logs or other detection type logs are associated with the respective investigation (e.g., ASIM logs, Government Sniffer Logs, etc.), they should be provided (electronic form preferable, paper is acceptable). This will enhance the examiner's ability to provide a better product and to interpret the logs in an effort to search for the right items.

NOTE: The examiner will conduct only the specific tasks requested. If not specified, then it will not be done. If obvious items are left off the request, the DCFL will call to verify. The more detail you provide, the better and more analysis we conduct.

NOTE: Contact your servicing computer expert to aid in creation of this request, if necessary.

9. ***AUTHORITY: Please indicate the legal basis for DCFL conducting the search you are requesting. There are generally three bases in criminal cases that would allow DCFL to perform your request:

1. Search Warrant/Military Search Authority [include supporting affidavits].

2. Consent.

   - DoD Banner.

   - Unit User Agreement.

   - Written Consent Signed by Authorizer.

   - Written Record of the Designated Approval Authority or Other Official who has the Right to Consent to the Search of the Media.

   - Memorandum of oral consent with special emphasis as to the scope of the consent granted.

3. Written Memo from servicing legal office stating that there is no reasonable expectation of privacy in the media submitted.

Inclusion of a copy of documents listed above is mandatory along with the request and will speed the analysis. Failure to include the same will result in a delay until such time as DCFL is satisfied that there is a legal basis for conducting the analysis.

10. ***OTHER DOCUMENTS: Requestors **MUST** provide the form used to open the investigation within their organization (e.g., provide a copy of an ACISS report, Army Form 66, or Navy ALS, etc.).

11. INSTRUCTIONS: Let the DCFL know if you have specific instructions. Please send copy of analysis report to both ? and ? Please return all evidence to ?

12. ***POC is: (This is the Requestor's contacting information, i.e., the person who authored this request. It could be the same as the "Lead Agent," and, if so, just state "Same."). Provide complete identification and contacting information: SA Jane Doe, AFOSI Detachment 999 at DSN: 123–1234 or Commercial: (123) 123–1234.

NOTE: If the required information (marked by ***) is not outlined in or not with this request, then the request for examination will be placed on hold until ALL information is provided.

JANE DOE, SA, USAF
Computer Crime Investigations

Example 3: Department of Maryland State Police Computer Forensic Laboratory

Department of Maryland State Police
Computer Forensic Laboratory

TELEPHONE 410-290-1620   FAX 410-290-1831

7155 C Columbia Gateway Drive, Columbia, Maryland 21046

REQUEST FOR SERVICE

Date Submitted:		MSP Complaint Control #:

Submitting Agency:	Address:	County:	Agency Case #:

Submitting Officer	ID#:	E-mail Address:	Telephone:

Location Seized:	Date Seized:	Agency Property #:

Case Title:	Suspect's Last Name, First Name, MI:	Sex: M F	Age:	Tracking Number:

Crime:	Date of Offense:	Date Charges Filed:	Court Date:	Court / Location:

Owner of Property - Name:	Address:	Telephone:

Type of Seizure: (Circle)   **Search Warrant**   **Consent**   **Administrative**   **Federal Grand Jury**   **Other:**

Number of Computers:	CCU Consulted Reference Seizure:	*(Attach a copy of the Search Warrant Affidavit and the Inventory/Return)*

Has this evidence been previoulsy viewed, accessed, and/or examined by anyone? (Explain)   **Yes**   **No**
Are you aware of any pirvileged information contained within the evidence being submitted for examination?   Explain)   **Yes**   **No**
Are you aware of any other information related to the evidence being submitted?   (Explain)   **Yes**   **No**

☐ **Urgent Request for Examination**

Date Request Received:	Person Making Request - Name / Title	Telephone # where you can be reached:	Date Analysis Needed:

Reason for Request: *(Except for Imminent Court dates, ALL Urgent requests must be accompanied by a letter of justification.)*

SERVICE REQUESTED: *(Requests for field service must be received at least 2 business days prior to search)*

INSTRUCTIONS

☐ Please prepare one form for each search site (address).
☐ Please provide **ALL** requested information and note any unusual circumstance in the "Service Requested" area.
☐ Please attach a **Request for Laboratory Examination Chain of Custody Log** (MSP Form 67) and a copy of your agency /installation **Property Record**, listing each container or package submitted as evidence.
☐ Please attach a **Detailed Summary** of suspect information, which includes personal data, e-mail addresses, nicknames, screen names, passwords, target websites, accomplices, and a list of unique keywords relevant to your investigation.

LABORATORY USE ONLY:		
LabCASE #:	**Date Case Received:** _____	**Case Priority:** 1 2 3 4 5
	Received by: _____	**Priority Established by:** _____

Appendix E. Legal Resources List

Publications

Searching and Seizing Computers and Obtaining Electronic Evidence in Criminal Investigations. Washington, D.C.: U.S. Department of Justice, Computer Crime and Intellectual Property Section, July 2002. (Online under http://www.cybercrime. gov/searching.html#A.)

Prosecuting Cases That Involve Computers: A Resource for State and Local Prosecutors (CD-ROM), National White Collar Crime Center, 2001. (See http://www.nctp.org and http://www. training.nw3c.org for information).

Forward Edge: Computer Training on Seizing Electronic Evidence (CD-ROM), U.S. Secret Service, 2001. (Contact your local U.S. Secret Service office.)

Legislation

Electronic Communications Privacy Act (ECPA). 18 USC 2510 et seq.; 18 USC 2701 et seq.; 18 USC 3121 et seq.

Privacy Protection Act (PPA). 42 USC 2000aa et seq.

USA PATRIOT ACT of 2001, Public Law 107-56, amended statutes relevant to computer investigations. Statutes amended include 18 USC 1030; 18 USC 2510 et seq.; 18 USC 2701 et seq.; 18 USC 3121 et seq.; and 47 USC 551.

Web sites

Computer Crime and Intellectual Property Section of the U.S. Department of Justice, 202–514–1026, http://www.cybercrime.gov.

National Cybercrime Training Partnership, 877–628–7674, http://www.nctp.org.

http://www.forensicsweb.com/downloads/cfid/isplist/isplist.htm

Appendix F. Technical Resources List

National

Computer Analysis Response Team
FBI Laboratory
935 Pennsylvania Avenue N.W.
Washington, DC 20535
Phone: 202–324–9307
http://www.fbi.gov/hq/lab/org/cart.htm

High Tech Crime Consortium
International Headquarters
1506 North Stevens Street
Tacoma, WA 98406–3826
Phone: 253–752–2427
Fax: 253–752–2430
E-mail: admin@hightechcrimecops.org
http://www.HighTechCrimeCops.org

Information Systems Security
Association (ISSA)
7044 South 13th Street
Oak Creek, WI 53154
Phone: 800–370–4772
http://www.issa.org

Internal Revenue Service
Criminal Investigation Division
2433 South Kirkwood Court
Denver, CO 80222
Phone: 303–756–0646
http://www.treas.gov/irs/ci/index.htm

National Aeronautics and Space
Administration
Office of Inspector General
Computer Crimes Division
300 E Street S.W.
Washington, DC 20546
Phone: 202–358–2573
http://www.hq.nasa.gov/office/oig/hq

National Association of Attorneys
General
Computer Crime Point of Contact
750 First Street N.E.
Suite 1100
Washington, DC 20002
Phone: 202–326–6000
http://www.naag.org/issues/
    20010724-cc_list_bg.php

National Center for Forensic Science
University of Central Florida
P.O. Box 162367
Orlando, FL 32816
Phone: 407–823–6469
Fax: 407–823–3162
http://www.ncfs.ucf.org

National Criminal Justice Computer
Laboratory and Training Center
SEARCH Group, Inc.
7311 Greenhaven Drive, Suite 145
Sacramento, CA 95831
Phone: 916–392–2550
http://www.search.org

National Law Enforcement and
Corrections Technology Center
(NLECTC)–Northeast
26 Electronic Parkway
Rome, NY 13441
Phone: 888–338–0584
Fax: 315–330–4315
http://www.justnet.org

National Law Enforcement and Corrections Technology Center (NLECTC)–West
c/o The Aerospace Corporation
2350 East El Segundo Boulevard
El Segundo, CA 90245
Phone: 888–548–1618
Fax: 310–336–2227
http://www.justnet.org

National Railroad Passenger Corporation (NRPC) (AMTRAK)
Office of Inspector General
Office of Investigations
10 G Street N.E., Suite 3E–400
Washington, DC 20002
Phone: 202–906–4318
E-mail: oigagent@aol.com

National White Collar Crime Center
Computer Crime Section
1000 Technology Drive, Suite 2130
Fairmont, WV 26554
Phone: 877–628–7674
http://www.cybercrime.org

Scientific Working Group for Digital Evidence
http://www.swgde.org

Social Security Administration
Office of Inspector General
Electronic Crimes Team
4–S–1 Operations Building
6401 Security Boulevard
Baltimore, MD 21235
Phone: 410–966–4225
Fax: 410–965–5705
http://www.ssa.gov/oig

U.S. Army Criminal Investigation Laboratory
U.S. Army Criminal Investigation
  Command
4553 N. 2d Street
Forest Park, GA 30297–5122
Phone: 404–469–7486

U.S. Customs Service CyberSmuggling Center
11320 Random Hills, Suite 400
Fairfax, VA 22030
Phone: 703–293–8005
Fax: 703–293–9127
http://www.customs.ustreas.gov/xp/cgov/
  enforcement/investigative_priorities/
  c3fact_sheet.xml

U.S. Department of Defense
DoD Computer Forensics Laboratory
911 Elkridge Landing Road, Suite 300
Linthicum, MD 21090
Phone: 410–981–0100/877–981–3235
http://www.dcfl.gov

U.S. Department of Defense
Office of Inspector General
Defense Criminal Investigative Service
Computer Forensics Analysis Program
400 Army Navy Drive, Suite 901
Arlington, VA 22202
Phone: 703–604–8733
http://www.dodig.osd.mil/dcis/
  dcismain.html
http://www.dodig.osd.mil/dcis/CFAP

U.S. Department of Energy
Office of the Inspector General
Technology Crimes Section
1000 Independence Avenue, 5A–235
Washington, DC 20585
Phone: 202–586–9939
Fax: 202–586–0754
E-mail: tech.crime@hq.doe.gov
http://www.ig.doe.gov

U.S. Department of Justice
Bureau of Alcohol, Tobacco, Firearms
  and Explosives
Technical Support Division
Visual Information Branch
650 Massachusetts Avenue N.W.
Room 3220
Washington, DC 20226–0013
Phone: 202–927–8037
Fax: 202–927–8682

U.S. Department of Justice
Criminal Division
Computer Crime and Intellectual Property
  Section (CCIPS)
10th and Constitution Avenue N.W.
John C. Keeney Building, Suite 600
Washington, DC 20530
Phone: 202–514–1026
http://www.cybercrime.gov

U.S. Department of Justice
Drug Enforcement Administration
Digital Evidence Laboratory
10555 Furnace Road
Lorton, VA 22079
Phone: 703–495–6787
Fax: 703–495–6794

U.S. Department of Transportation
Office of Inspector General
200 West Adams, Suite 300
Chicago, IL 60606
Phone: 312–353–0106
Fax: 312–353–7032

U.S. Postal Inspection Service
Forensic and Technical Services Division
Digital Evidence
22433 Randolph Drive
Dulles, VA 20104–1000
Phone: 703–406–7927
http://www.usps.com/postalinspectors/
  crimelab.htm

U.S. Postal Service
Office of Inspector General
Technical Crime Unit
1735 North Lynn Street
Arlington, VA 22209–2020
Phone: 703–248–2100
http://www.uspsoig.gov

U.S. Secret Service
Electronic Crimes Branch
950 H Street N.W.
Washington, DC 20223
Phone: 202–406–5850
Fax: 202–406–9233
http://www.treas.gov/usss

Veterans Affairs
Office of the Inspector General
Computer Crimes and Forensics
801 I Street N.W., Suite 1064
Washington, DC 20001
Phone: 202–565–5701
http://www.va.gov/oig/homepage.htm

By State

Alabama

Alabama Attorney General's Office
Donna White
Special Agent
11 South Union Street
Montgomery, AL 36130
Phone: 334–242–7345
Fax: 334–242–0928
E-mail: dwhite@ago.state.al.us
http://www.ago.state.al.us

Alabama Bureau of Investigation
Internet Crimes Against Children Unit
Glenn Taylor
Agent
716 Arcadia Circle
Huntsville, AL 35801
Phone: 256–539–4028
E-mail: tgtjr@aol.com

Homewood Police Department
Wade Morgan
1833 29th Avenue South
Homewood, AL 35209
Phone: 205–877–8637
E-mail: morgan64@bellsouth.net

Hoover Police Department
Sgt. Harry Long
100 Municipal Drive
Hoover, AL 35216
Phone: 205–444–7533
E-mail: longh@ci.hoover.al.us
http://www.hooveral.org/content/police/
  policeand911.htm

Alaska

Alaska State Troopers
Sgt. Curt Harris
White Collar Crime Section
5700 East Tudor Road
Anchorage, AK 99507
Phone: 907–269–5627
Fax: 907–269–5493
E-mail: curtis_harris@dps.state.ak.us
http://www.dps.state.ak.us/ast

Anchorage Police Department
Det. Glen Klinkhart/Sgt. Ross Plummer
4501 South Bragaw Street
Anchorage, AK 99507–1599
Phone: 907–786–8767/907–786–8778
E-mail: gklinkhart@ci.anchorage.ak.us
rplummer@ci.us.ak.gov
http://www.ci.anchorage.ak.us/apd

University of Alaska at Fairbanks Police Department
Officer Marc Poeschel
Interior Alaska FORCES (IAF) Task
  Coordinator
P.O. Box 755560
Fairbanks, AK 99775–5560
Phone: 907–474–6200
E-mail: fyglock@uaf.edu
http://www.akforces.uaf.edu

Arizona

Arizona Attorney General's Office
Gail Thackeray
Assistant Attorney General
Technology Crimes Unit
1275 West Washington Street
Phoenix, AZ 85007
Phone: 602–542–3881
Fax: 602–542–5997
E-mail: gail.thackeray@ag.state.az.us
Special Agent William Sutter, CFCE
Phone: 602–542–4853
Fax: 602–542–4882
E-mail: william.sutter@ag.state.az.us
http://www.ag.state.az.us

Arizona Regional Computer Forensic Laboratory
Sgt. R. Hopper
P.O. Box 6638
Phoenix, AZ 85005
Phone: 602–223–2698
Fax: 602–223–2332

Arkansas

University of Arkansas at Little Rock Police Department
William (Bill) Reardon/Bobby Floyd
2801 South University Avenue
Little Rock, AR 72204
Phone: 501–569–8793/501–569–8794
E-mail: wcreardon@ualr.edu
bcfloyd@ualr.edu

California

Bay Area Electronic Crimes Task Force
Don Wilborn/SA Susan Broad
345 Spear Street
San Francisco, CA 94105
Phone: 415–744–9026
Fax: 415–744–9051
E-mail: dwilborn@usss.treas.gov

California Department of Justice
Bureau of Medi-Cal Fraud and Elder Abuse
Luis Salazar
Senior Legal Analyst/Computer Forensic
  Examiner
1455 Frazee Road, Suite 315
San Diego, CA 92108
Phone: 619–688–6182
Fax: 619–688–4200
E-mail: Luis.Salazar@doj.ca.gov
http://www.caag.state.ca.us/bmfea

California Franchise Tax Board
Investigations Bureau
Ashraf L. Massoud
Senior Special Agent
100 North Barranca Street, Suite 500
West Covina, CA 91791–1600
Phone: 626–859–4678
E-mail: ashraf_massoud@ftb.ca.gov

Kern County Sheriff's Department
Tom Fugitt
1350 Norris Road
Bakersfield, CA 93308
Phone: 661–391–7453
E-mail: fugitt@co.kern.ca.us
http://www.co.kern.ca.us/sheriff/rcfl.htm

Los Angeles Police Department
Computer Crime Unit
Det. Terry D. Willis
150 North Los Angeles Street
Los Angeles, CA 90012
Phone: 213–485–3795
http://www.lapd.org

Modesto Police Department
Computer Forensics Unit
600 10th Street
Modesto, CA 95354
Phone: 209–572–9500, ext. 29119
http://www.ci.modesto.ca.us/mpd/
  departments/computer%5Ffor.htm

**Northern California Computer Crimes
Task Force**
Sgt. Dave Bettin
455 Devlin Road, Suite 207
Napa, CA 94559
Phone: 707–253–4500

**Regional Computer Forensic Laboratory
at San Diego**
Sgt. Rusty Sargent
Operations Manager
9797 Aero Drive
San Diego, CA 92123–1800
Phone: 858–499–7799
Fax: 858–499–7798
E-mail: rcfl@rcfl.org
http://www.rcfl.org

**Sacramento Valley Hi-Tech Crimes
Task Force**
Hi-Tech Crimes Division
Sacramento County Sheriff's Department
Lt. Mike Tsuchida
4510 Orange Grove Avenue
Sacramento, CA 95841
Phone: 916–874–3030
E-mail: mtsuchida@sacsheriff.com
http://www.sacsheriff.com

**San Diego High Technology Crimes
Economic Fraud Division**
David Decker
District Attorney's Office, County of
  San Diego
Suite 750
San Diego, CA 92101
Phone: 619–531–3660
E-mail: ddecke@sdcda.org

**Silicon Valley High Tech Crime
Task Force**
Rapid Enforcement Allied Computer Team
  (REACT)
c/o Federal Bureau of Investigation
Nick Muyo
950 South Bascom Avenue, Suite 3011
San Jose, CA 95128
Phone: 408–494–7161
Pager: 408–994–3264
E-mail: sharx91@aol.com

Southern California High Technology Task Force
Lt. Rick Craigo
Commercial Crimes Bureau
Los Angeles County Sheriff's Department
12440 East Imperial Highway, Suite B130
Norwalk, CA 90650
Phone: 562–345–4260

United States Secret Service
Los Angeles Electronic Crimes
Task Force
725 South Figueroa Street, Suite 1300
Los Angeles, CA 90017–5418
Phone: 213–894–4830 or 213–533–4650
Fax: 213–533–4729
E-mail: laxectf@usss.treas.gov
ATSAIC Donald Masters
Phone: 213–533–4691
E-mail: laxectf@usss.treas.gov
ATSAIC John "Keith" Helton
Phone: 213–533–4651
E-mail: jhelton@usss.treas.gov

U.S. Customs Service
Frank Day
Senior Special Agent
Computer Investigative Specialist
3403 10th Street, Suite 600
Riverside, CA 92501
Phone: 909–276–6664, ext. 231
E-mail: FDay@usa.net

Colorado

Colorado Regional Computer Forensic Laboratory
John Davis
Operations Manager
9350 Heritage Hills Circle
Lone Tree, CO 80124
Phone: 303–784–7814
Fax: 303–790–4124
E-mail: jtdavis@douglas.co.us

Denver District Attorney's Office
Henry R. Reeve
General Counsel/Deputy D.A.
201 West Colfax Avenue, Dept. 801
Denver, CO 80202
Phone: 720–913–9000
E-mail: htr@denverdq.org
http://www.denverda.org

Department of Public Safety
Colorado Bureau of Investigation
Computer Crime Investigation
710 Kipling Street, Suite 200
Denver, CO 80215
Phone: 303–239–4292
Fax: 303–239–5788
E-mail: Collin.Reese@cdps.state.co.us
http://cbi.state.co.us

Connecticut

Connecticut Department of Public Safety
Division of Scientific Services
Forensic Science Laboratory
Computer Crimes and Electronic
 Evidence Unit
278 Colony Street
Meriden, CT 06451
Phone: 203–639–6492
Fax: 203–630–3760
E-mail: agr.ccu@snet.net
http://www.state.ct.us/DPS/DSS/
 ComputerCrimes.htm

Connecticut Department of Revenue Services
Special Investigations Section
25 Sigourney Street
Hartford, CT 06106
Phone: 860–297–5877
Fax: 860–297–5625
http://www.drs.state.ct.us

Yale University Police Department
Sgt. Dan Rainville
98–100 Sachem Street
New Haven, CT 06511
Phone: 203–432–7958
E-mail: daniel.rainville@yale.edu
http://www.yale.edu/police

Delaware

Delaware State Police
High Technology Crimes Unit
1575 McKee Road, Suite 204
Dover, DE 19904
Det. Steve Whalen
Phone: 302–739–2761
E-mail: Steve.Whalen@state.de.us
Det. Daniel Willey
Phone: 302–739–8020
E-mail: Daniel.Willey@state.de.us
Sgt. Robert Moses
Phone: 302–739–2467
E-mail: Bob.Moses@state.de.us
Sgt. Kevin Perna
Phone: 302–739–1399
E-mail: kperna@state.de.us
http://www.state.de.us/dsp

New Castle County Police Department
Criminal Investigations Unit
Det. Christopher M. Shanahan/
Det. Edward E. Whatley/Det. Joseph Trala
3601 North DuPont Highway
New Castle, DE 19720
Phone: 302–395–8110
E-mail: cshanahan@co.new-castle.de.us
eewhatley@co.new-castle.de.us
jtrala@co.new-castle.de.us
http://www.nccpd.com

University of Delaware Police Department
Capt. Stephen M. Bunting
101 MOB
700 Pilottown Road
Lewes, DE 19958
Phone: 302–645–4334
E-mail: sbunting@udel.edu

District of Columbia

Metropolitan Police Department
Special Investigations Branch
Computer Crimes and Forensics Unit
Investigator Tim Milloff
300 Indiana Avenue N.W., Room 3019
Washington, DC 20001
Phone: 202–727–4723/202–727–1010
Fax: 202–727–2398
E-mail: tmilloff@mpdc.org
http://mpdc.dc.gov

Washington Metropolitan Electronic Crimes Task Force
1100 L Street N.W.
Washington, DC 20003
Phone: 202–406–8500
Fax: 202–406–8503

Florida

Florida Atlantic University Police Department

Det. Wilfredo Hernandez
777 Glades Road, #49
Boca Raton, FL 33431
Phone: 561–297–2371
Fax: 561–297–0144
E-mail: hernande@fau.edu
http://www.fau.edu/police

Gainesville Police Department
Criminal Investigations/Computer Unit
721 N.W. Sixth Street
Gainesville, FL 32601
Phone: 352–334–2471
Fax: 352–334–3232
http://www.gainesvillepd.org

Institute of Police Technology and Management
Computer Forensics Laboratory
University of North Florida
12000 Alumni Drive
Jacksonville, FL 32224–2678
Phone: 904–620–4786
Fax: 904–620–2453
http://www.iptm.org

Miami Electronic Crimes Task Force
ATSAIC Alex Echo
8375 N.W. 53rd Street
Miami, FL 33166
Phone: 305–629–1800
Fax: 305–629–1830
E-mail: aecho@usss.treas.gov

Office of Statewide Prosecution
High Technology Crimes
Thomas A. Sadaka
Special Counsel
135 West Central Boulevard, Suite 1000
Orlando, FL 32801
Phone: 407–245–0893
Fax: 407–245–0356
E-mail: thomas_sadaka@oag.state.fl.us
http://legal.firn.edu/swp/index.html

Pinellas County Sheriff's Office
Det. Matthew Miller
10750 Ulmerton Road
Largo, FL 33778
Phone: 727–582–6345
E-mail: mmiller@pcsonet.com
http://www.co.pinellas.fl.us/sheriff

Georgia

Georgia Bureau of Investigation
Financial Investigations Unit
Steve Edwards
Special Agent in Charge
5255 Snapfinger Drive, Suite 150
Decatur, GA 30035
Phone: 770–987–2323
Fax: 770–987–9775
E-mail: steve.edwards@gbi.state.ga.us
http://www.ganet.org/gbi

Hawaii

Honolulu Police Department
White Collar Crime Unit
Det. Chris Duque
801 South Beretania Street
Honolulu, HI 96813
Phone: 808–529–3112

Idaho

Ada County Sheriff's Office
Det. Lon Anderson, CFCE
7200 Barrister Drive
Boise, ID 83704
Phone: 208–377–6691
http://www.adasheriff.org

Illinois

Chicago Electronic Crimes Task Force (CECTF)
Paul Wattay
Supervisor
Assistant to the Special Agent in Charge
525 West Van Buren Street, Suite 900
Chicago, IL 60607
Phone: 312–353–5431
Fax: 312–353–1225
E-mail: pwattay@usss.treas.gov

Chicago Regional Computer Forensics Laboratory
610 South Canal Street, Fifth Floor
Chicago, IL 60607
Phone: 312–913–9270
Fax: 312–913–9408
http://www.chicagorcfl.org

Illinois Attorney General's Office
High Tech Crimes Bureau
Keith Chval, Chief
188 West Randolph
Chicago, IL 60601
Phone: 312–814–3762
Fax: 312–814–8283
E-mail: kchval@atg.state.il.us

Illinois State Police
Electronic Investigation Unit
Division of Operations
Operational Services Command
Statewide Support Bureau
500 Illes Park Place, Suite 104
Springfield, IL 62718
Phone: 217–785–0631
Fax: 217–785–6793
http://www.isp.state.il.us

Illinois State Police
Electronic Investigations Section
Master Sgt. James Murray
8151 West 183rd Street, Suite F
Tinley Park, IL 60477
Phone: 708–633–5561
E-mail: murrayj@isp.state.il.us
http://www.isp.state.il.us

Tazewell County State's Attorney CID
Det. Dave Frank
342 Court Street, Suite 6
Pekin, IL 61554–3298
Phone: 309–477–2205, ext. 400
Fax: 309–477–2729
E-mail: sainv@tazewell.com

Indiana

Evansville Police Department
Det. J. Walker/Det. Craig Jordan
15 N.W. Martin Luther King, Jr., Boulevard
Evansville, IN 47708
Phone: 812–436–7995/812–436–7994
E-mail: Jwalker@evansvillepolice.com
cjordan@evansvillepolice.com
http://www.evansvillepolice.com

Indiana State Police
Det. David L. Lloyd
Computer Crime Unit
5811 Ellison Road
Fort Wayne, IN 46750
Phone: 765–662–9864, ext. 174
E-mail: ispdet@aol.com
http://www.ai.org/isp

Indianapolis Police Department
Det. William J. Howard
901 North Post Road, Room 115
Indianapolis, IN 46219
Phone: 317–327–3461
E-mail: vulcan@netdirect.net
http://www.indygov.org/ipd

Iowa

Iowa Division of Criminal Investigation
920 Southwest Morgan Street, Suite G
Des Moines, IA 50309
Phone: 515–281–7671
Fax: 515–281–7638
http://www.state.ia.us/government/dps/dci

Kansas

Kansas Bureau of Investigation
High Technology Crime Investigation Unit
  (HTCIU)
David J. Schroeder
Senior Special Agent
1620 S.W. Tyler Street
Topeka, KS 66612–1837
Phone: 785–296–8222
Fax: 785–296–0525
E-mail: dave.schroeder@kbi.state.ks.us
http://www.accesskansas.org/kbi/
  main.html

Olathe Police Department
Det. Patrick Foster
501 East 56 Highway
Olathe, KS 66061
Phone: 913–971–6542
Fax: 913–782–3127
E-mail: PFoster@olatheks.org
http://www.olatheks.org/Public_Safety/
  Police/index.cfm

Wichita Police Department
Forensic Computer Crimes Unit
Det. Shaun Price/Det. Brett Eisenman
130 South Market Street
Wichita, KS 67202
Phone: 316–337–6124
E-mail: sprice@sedgwick.gov
beisenma@sedgwick.gov
http://www.wichitapolice.com

Kentucky

Boone County Sheriff
Capt. Jack Prindle
P.O. Box 198
Burlington, KY 41005
Phone: 859–334–2175
E-mail: jprindle@boonecountyky.org

Louisiana

Gonzales Police Department
Officer Dan Crummey
120 South Irma Boulevard
Gonzales, LA 70737
Phone: 225–647–9535
Fax: 225–647–9544

Louisiana Department of Justice
Criminal Division
High Technology Crime Unit
339 Florida Street, Suite 402
Baton Rouge, LA 70801
James L. Piker, Assistant Attorney General
Section Chief, High Technology Crime Unit
Investigator Clayton Rives
Phone: 225–342–7552
Fax: 225–342–7893
E-mail: PikerJ@ag.state.la.us
RivesCS@ag.state.la.us
Scott Turner, Computer Forensic Examiner
Phone: 225–342–4060
Fax: 225–342–3482
E-mail: TurnerS@ag.state.la.us
http://www.ag.state.la.us

Maine

Maine Computer Crimes Task Force
171 Park Street
Lewiston, ME 04240
Det. James C. Rioux
Phone: 207–784–6422, ext. 250
Investigator Mike Webber
Phone: 207–784–6422, ext. 255
Det. Thomas Bureau
Phone: 207–784–6422, ext. 256
http://www.mcctf.org

Maryland

Anne Arundel County Police Department
Computer Analysis Unit
Det. Bob Reyes
41 Community Place
Crownsville, MD 21032
Phone: 410–222–3409
E-mail: breyesjr1@yahoo.com
http://www.aacopd.org

Department of Maryland State Police
Technical Assistance and Computer
 Crimes Division
Lt. Barry E. Leese
Division Commander
7155–C Columbia Gateway Drive
Columbia, MD 21046
Phone: 410–290–1620
Fax: 410–290–1831
E-mail: bleese@mdsp.org

Montgomery County Police
Computer Crime Unit
2350 Research Boulevard
Rockville, MD 20850
Phone: 301–840–2590
E-mail: mcpdccu@montgomery
 countymd.gov
http://www.co.mo.md.us/services/police/
 ccu/computercrime.htm

Massachusetts

Massachusetts Office of the Attorney General
Corruption, Fraud, and Computer Crime
  Division
John Grossman, Chief
Assistant Attorney General
One Ashburton Place
Boston, MA 02108
Phone: 617–727–2200
http://www.ago.state.ma.us

New England Electronic Crimes Task Force
10 Causeway Street, No. 791
Boston, MA 02222
Phone: 617–565–6642 or 617–565–5640
Fax: 617–565–5103
http://www.neectf.org

Michigan

Michigan Department of Attorney General
High Tech Crime Unit
18050 Deering
Livonia, MI 48152
Phone: 734–525–4151
Fax: 734–525–4372
E-mail: miag-htu@michigan.gov
http://www.ag.state.mi.us

Oakland County Sheriff's Department
Computer Crimes Unit
Det. Carol Liposky
1201 North Telegraph Road
Pontiac, MI 48341
Phone: 248–452–9843
Fax: 248–858–9565
http://www.co.oakland.mi.us/c_serv/ocsd

Minnesota

Ramsey County Sheriff's Department
Deputy Mike O'Neill
14 West Kellogg Boulevard
St. Paul, MN 55102
Phone: 651–266–2797
E-mail: mike.oneill@co.ramsey.mn.us
http://www.ramseycountysheriff.org

Mississippi

Biloxi Police Department
Investigator Donnie G. Dobbs
170 Porter Avenue
Biloxi, MS 39530
Phone: 228–435–6112
E-mail: mgc2d11@aol.com
http://www.biloxi.ms.us/
  police_department.html

Missouri

St. Louis Metropolitan Police Department
High Tech Crimes Unit
Det. Sgt. Robert Muffler
1200 Clark
St. Louis, MO 63102
Phone: 314–444–5441
Fax: 314–444–5432
E-mail: rjmuffler@slmpd.org
http://www.stlouiscitypolicedept.org

Montana

Montana Division of Criminal Investigation
Computer Crime Unit
Jimmy Weg, CFCE
Agent in Charge
303 North Roberts, Room 371
Helena, MT 59620
Phone: 406–444–6681
Cell phone: 406–439–6185
E-mail: jweg@state.mt.us
http://www.doj.state.mt.us/enforcement/
  default.asp

Nebraska

Lincoln Police Department
Investigator Ed Sexton
575 South 10th Street
Lincoln, NE 68508
Phone: 402–441–7587
E-mail: lpd358@cjis.ci.lincoln.ne.us
http://www.ci.lincoln.ne.us/city/police/

Nebraska State Patrol
Internet Crimes Against Children Unit
Sgt. Scott Christensen
Coordinator
4411 South 108th Street
Omaha, NE 68137
Phone: 402–595–2410
Fax: 402–595–3303
E-mail: schriste@nsp.state.ne.us
http://www.nsp.state.ne.us

Nevada

City of Reno, Nevada, Police Department
Computer Crimes Unit
455 East Second Street
Reno, NV 89502
P.O. Box 1900 (mailing address)
Reno, NV 89505
Phone: 775–334–2107
Fax: 775–785–4026
http://www.cityofreno.com/pub_safety/
  police

Las Vegas Electronic Crimes Task Force
SA James Darnell
600 Las Vegas Boulevard South, Suite 700
Las Vegas, NV 89101
Phone: 702–388–6571
Fax: 702–388–6668
E-mail: jdarnell@usss.treas.gov

Nevada Attorney General's Office
John Lusak
Senior Computer Forensic Tech
1325 Airmotive Way, Suite 340
Reno, NV 89501
Phone: 775–328–2889
E-mail: jlusak@govmail.state.nv.us
http://www.ag.state.nv.us

New Hampshire

New Hampshire State Police Forensic Laboratory
Computer Crimes Unit
10 Hazen Drive
Concord, NH 03305
Phone: 603–271–0300
http://www.state.nh.us/safety/nhsp

New Jersey

New Jersey Division of Criminal Justice
Computer Analysis and Technology Unit
  (CATU)
James Parolski
Supervising State Investigator
P.O. Box 085
25 Market Street
Trenton, NJ 08625–0085
Phone: 609–984–5256/609–984–6500
Pager: 888–819–1292
E-mail: parolskij@njdj.org
http://www.state.nj.us/lps/dcj/catunit.htm

Ocean County Prosecutor's Office
Special Investigations Unit/Computer
  Crimes
Investigator Mike Nevil
P.O. Box 2191
Toms River, NJ 08753
Phone: 732–929–2027, ext. 4014
Fax: 732–349–4291
E-mail: mnevil@co.ocean.nj.us
http://www.co.ocean.nj.us/prosecutor/
  main.htm

New Mexico

New Mexico Gaming Control Board
Information Systems Division
Donovan Lieurance
6400 Uptown Boulevard N.E., Suite 100E
Albuquerque, NM 87110
Phone: 505–841–9719
Fax: 505–841–9773
E-mail: dlieurance@nmgcb.org
http://www.nmgcb.org

Twelfth Judicial District Attorney's Office
Investigator Jack Henderson
1000 New York Avenue, Room 301
Alamogordo, NM 88310
Phone: 505–437–1313, ext. 110
E-mail: jdh@zianet.com

New York

Erie County Sheriff's Office
Computer Crime Unit
10 Delaware Avenue
Buffalo, NY 14202
Phone: 716–662–6150
http://www.erie.gov/sheriff/
    CCU_contact.asp

John Jay College of Criminal Justice
The City University of New York
Stephen E. Smith Center for Cyber Crime
555 West 57th Street, Suite 601
New York, NY 10019
Phone: 212–237–8489
E-mail: wmoylan@jjay.cuny.edu
http://www.jjay.cuny.edu/
    centersInstitutes/cyberctr/

Nassau County Police Department
Computer Crime Section
Det. Bill Moylan
970 Brush Hollow Road
Westbury, NY 11590
Phone: 516–573–5275
E-mail: billyfm@aol.com
http://www.co.nassau.ny.us/police/

New York Electronic Crimes Task Force
United States Secret Service
Robert Weaver
Deputy Special Agent in Charge
335 Adams Street, 32nd Floor
Brooklyn, NY 11201
Phone: 718–625–1385
Fax: 718–625–6708
E-mail: rweaver@usss.treas.gov

New York Police Department
Computer Investigation and Technology
    Unit
1 Police Plaza, Room 1112
New York, NY 10038
Phone: 646–610–5397
Fax: 646–610–6216
E-mail: citu@nypd.org
http://NYC.gov/html/nypd/html/db/citujd.
    html

New York State Attorney General's Office
Internet Bureau
120 Broadway
New York, NY 10271
Phone: 212–416–8433
http://www.oag.state.ny.us

New York State Department of Taxation and Finance
Office of Deputy Inspector General
W.A. Harriman Campus
Building 9, Room 481
Albany, NY 12227
Phone: 518–485–8698
http://www.tax.state.ny.us

New York State Police
Computer Crime Unit
Lt. Ronald R. Stevens
Forensic Investigation Center
Building 30, State Campus
1220 Washington Avenue
Albany, NY 12226
Phone: 518–457–5712
Fax: 518–402–2773
E-mail: nyspccu@troopers.state.ny.us
http://www.troopers.state.ny.us/
  CrimInv/ComputerCrime.html

**Regional Computer Forensics
Lab–Western New York**
4455 Genesee Street
Cheektowaga, NY 14225
Phone: 716–631–0261
http://www.rcflwny.org

Rockland County Sheriff's Department
Computer Crime Task Force
Det. Lt. John J. Gould
55 New Hempstead Road
New City, NY 10956
Phone: 845–708–7860/845–638–5836
Fax: 845–708–7821
E-mail: gouldjo@co.rockland.ny.us
http://www.co.rockland.ny.us/Sheriff/
  default.htm

North Carolina

**Charlotte Metro Electronic Financial
Crimes Task Force**
ATSAIC Ignacio Marino
One Fairview Center
6302 Fairview Road
Charlotte, NC 28210
Phone: 704–442–8370
Fax: 704–442–8369
E-mail: imarino@usss.treas.gov

Raleigh Police Department
Investigator Patrick Niemann
110 South McDowell Street
Raleigh, NC 27601
Phone: 919–890–3555
E-mail: niemannp@raleigh-nc.org
http://www.raleigh-nc.org/police/index.htm

North Dakota

**North Dakota Bureau of Criminal
Investigation**
Tim J. Erickson
Special Agent
P.O. Box 1054
Bismarck, ND 58502–1054
Phone: 701–328–5500
E-mail: te409@state.nd.us
http://www.ag.state.nd.us/BCI/BCI.html

Ohio

Hamilton County Ohio Sheriff's Office
Maj. Bruce Knox
Justice Center
1000 Sycamore Street, Room 110
Cincinnati, OH 45202
Phone: 513–946–6651
Fax: 513–946–6690
http://www.hcso.org
  (under the Administration Division)

Ohio Attorney General's Office
Bureau of Criminal Investigation
Computer Crime Unit
Kathleen Barch
Criminal Investigation Administrator
1560 State Route 56
London, OH 43140
Phone: 740–845–2410
E-mail: KBarch@ag.state.oh.us
http://www.ag.state.oh.us

Riverside Police Department
Officer Harold Jones
MCSE/Computer Crime Specialist
1791 Harshman Road
Riverside, OH 45424
Phone: 937–238–8064/937–233–1820
E-mail: hjones@cops.org
harold@search.org

Oklahoma

Oklahoma Attorney General
4545 North Lincoln Boulevard
Suite 260
Oklahoma City, OK 73105–3498
Phone: 405–521–4274
E-mail: jim_powell@oag.state.ok.us
http://www.oag.state.ok.us

Oklahoma State Bureau of Investigation
Mark R. McCoy, Ed.D., CFCE
Deputy Inspector
6600 North Harvey
Oklahoma City, OK 73116
Phone: 405–848–6724
Fax: 405–879–2622
E-mail: markm@osbi.state.ok.us
http://www.osbi.state.ok.us

Oregon

Deschutes County Sheriff's Office
Computer Crimes Detail
Sgt. Tom Nelson
Computer Forensics Specialist
63333 West Highway 20
Bend, OR 97701
Phone: 541–322–4811
E-mail: Tom_Nelson@co.deschutes.or.us

Gresham Police Department
Rich Boyd
Computer Forensic Investigator
1333 N.W. Eastman Parkway
Gresham, OR 97030
Phone: 503–666–1997
Fax: 503–665–1693
E-mail: boyd_r@ci.gresham.or.us

Oregon High-Tech Team
Joel Brillhart
Special Agent
FBI
20795 N.W. Cornell, Suite 100
Hillsboro, OR 97124
Phone: 503–615–6627
E-mail: joelb@ci.hillsboro.or.us

Oregon State Police
Det. Steve Payne
4760 Portland Road N.E.
Salem, OR 97305
Phone: 503–378–2110, ext. 409
Det. Randy Becker
4500 Rogue Valley Highway, Suite B
Central Point, OR 97502
Phone: 541–776–6114, ext. 243
http://www.osp.state.or.us

Portland Police Bureau
Computer Forensics Detail
Sgt. Randy Day
Supervisor
1111 S.W. Second Avenue, Room 1326
Portland, OR 97204
Phone: 503–823–0400
E-mail: rday@police.ci.portland.or.us
http://www.portlandpolicebureau.com/

Washington County Sheriff's Office
Computer Forensic Investigations
Brian Budlong
215 S.W. Adams Avenue, MS32
Hillsboro, OR 97123
Phone: 503–846–2573
Fax: 503–846–2637
E-mail: brian_budlong@co.washington.
  or.us
http://www.co.washington.or.us/cgi/
  sheriff/lec.pl

Pennsylvania

Allegheny County Police Department
High Tech Crime Unit
Det. T. Haney
400 North Lexington Street
Pittsburgh, PA 15208
Phone: 412–473–1304
Fax: 412–473–1377
E-mail: thaney@county.allegheny.pa.us
http://www.county.allegheny.pa.us/police/

Erie County District Attorney's Office
Erie County Courthouse
140 West Sixth Street
Erie, PA 16501
Phone: 814–451–6349
Fax: 814–451–6419

Rhode Island

Warwick Police Department
Detective Division
Det. Edmund Pierce
99 Veterans Memorial Drive
Warwick, RI 02886
Phone: 401–468–4200 (main)/
401–468–4263 (direct)
Fax: 401–468–4265
E-mail: WPDDetectives@cox.com
  efp31@cox.net
http://www.warwickpd.org

South Carolina

**South Carolina Law Enforcement
Division (SLED)**
South Carolina Computer Crime Center
Lt. L.J. "Chip" Johnson
Supervisory Special Agent
P.O. Box 21398
Columbia, SC 29221–1398
Phone: 803–737–9000
http://www.sled.state.sc.us/

Winthrop University
Winthrop Police Department
Daniel R. Yeargin
Assistant Chief of Police
2 Crawford Building
Rock Hill, SC 29733
Phone: 803–323–3496
E-mail: yeargind@winthrop.edu
http://www.winthrop.edu/publicsafety/

South Dakota

**South Dakota Internet Crimes
Enforcement**
Robert Grandpre
Assistant Director DCI
Office of the Attorney General
Division of Criminal Investigation
3444 East Highway 34
c/o 500 East Capitol Avenue
Pierre, SD 57501–5070
Phone: 605–773–3331
Fax: 605–773–4629
E-mail: robertgrandpre@state.sd.us

Tennessee

Harriman Police Department
130 Pansy Hill Road
P.O. Drawer 433 (mailing address)
Harriman, TN 37748
Phone: 865–882–3383
Fax: 865–882–0700
E-mail: harrimanpd@comcast.net

Knox County Sheriff's Office
Carleton Bryant
Staff Attorney
400 West Main Avenue
Knoxville, TN 37902
Phone: 865–971–3911
E-mail: sheriff@esper.com
http://www.knoxsheriff.org/

Tennessee Attorney General's Office
David Neal
Forensic Technology Investigator
425 Fifth Avenue, North
Nashville, TN 37243
Phone: 615–532–9658
E-mail: david.neal@state.tn.us
http://www.attorneygeneral.state.tn.us/

Texas

Austin Police Department
715 East Eighth Street
Austin, TX 78701
http://www.ci.austin.tx.us/police

Bexar County District Attorney's Office
Russ Brandau/David Getrost
300 Dolorosa
San Antonio, TX 78205
Phone: 210–335–2368/210–335–2991
E-mail: rbrandau@co.bexar.tx.us
dgetrost@co.bexar.tx.us
http://www.co.bexar.tx.us/da/

Dallas Police Department
2014 Main Street
Dallas, TX 75201
http://www.dallaspolice.net

Federal Bureau of Investigation Dallas Field Office
One Justice Way
J. Gordon Shanklin Building
Dallas, TX 75220
Phone: 972–559–5000
http://dallas.fbi.gov

Houston Police Department
1200 Travis Street
Houston, TX 77002
http://www.ci.houston.tx.us/departme/
  police

Office of the Attorney General
Internet Bureau
P.O. Box 12548
Austin, TX 78711–2548
Phone: 512–936–2899
http://www.oag.state.tx.us
http://www.texasinternetbureau.com

Portland Police Department
Det. Terrell Elliott
902 Moore Avenue
Portland, TX 78374
Phone: 361–643–2546
Fax: 361–643–5689
E-mail: telliott@portlandpd.com
http://www.portlandpd.com

Texas Department of Public Safety
5805 North Lamar Boulevard
Austin, TX 78752–4422
P.O. Box 4087 (mailing address)
Austin, TX 78773–0001
Phone: 512–424–2200/800–252–5402
E-mail: specialcrimes@txdps.state.tx.us
http://www.txdps.state.tx.us

Utah

Utah Department of Public Safety
State Bureau of Investigations, Forensic
Computer Lab
Daniel D. Hooper
Special Agent
3888 West 5400 South
Kearns, UT 84118
Phone: 801–955–2121
E-mail: dhooper@utah.gov

Vermont

**State of Vermont Department of
Public Safety**
Bureau of Criminal Investigation
Sgt. Mark Lauer
103 South Main Street
Waterbury, VT 05671–2101
Phone: 802–241–5367
Fax: 802–241–5349
E-mail: mlauer@dps.state.vt.us
http://www.dps.state.vt.us/vtsp

Vermont Internet Crimes Task Force
Lt. Michael Schirling
Burlington Police
1 North Avenue
Burlington, VT 05401
Phone: 802–658–2704, ext. 131
E-mail: mschirling@bpdvt.org

Virginia

Arlington County Police Department
Criminal Investigations Division
Computer Forensics
Det. Ray Rimer
1425 North Courthouse Road
Arlington, VA 22201
Phone: 703–228–7994
Pager: 703–866–8965
E-mail: rimer550@erols.com
cfu550@aol.com
http://www.co.arlington.va.us/police/

Fairfax County Police Department
Computer Forensics Section
Lt. Dave Russell
4100 Chain Bridge Road
Fairfax, VA 22030
Phone: 703–246–7867
Fax: 703–246–4253
http://www.co.fairfax.va.us/ps/police/
  homepage.htm

Richmond Police Department
Technology Crimes Section
Det. Jeff Deem
200 West Grace Street
Richmond, VA 23220
Phone: 804–646–3949
Fax: 804–646–4880
E-mail: jdeem@ci.richmond.va.us
http://www.ci.richmond.va.us/police/

Virginia Beach Police Department
Det. Michael Encarnacao
Special Investigations CERU
2509 Princess Anne Road
Virginia Beach, VA 23456
Phone: 757–427–1749
E-mail: mikee@cops.org
http://www.vbgov.com

Virginia Department of Motor Vehicles
Law Enforcement Section
Larry L. Barnett
Assistant Special Agent in Charge
945 Edwards Ferry Road N.E.
Leesburg, VA 20176
Phone: 703–771–4757
E-mail: lbtrip@erols.com

Virginia Office of the Attorney General
Addison L. Cheeseman
Senior Criminal Investigator
900 East Main Street
Richmond, VA 23219
Phone: 804–786–6554
E-mail: acheeseman@oag.state.va.us
http://www.oag.state.va.us/

Virginia State Police
Andrew Clark, CFCE
Computer Technology Specialist 3
Richmond, VA 23236
Phone: 804–323–2040
E-mail: AndyClark@att.net
http://www.vsp.state.va.us

Washington

King County Sheriff's Office
Fraud/Computer Investigations Unit
Sgt. Steve Davis/Det. Brian Palmer
401 Fourth Avenue North, RJC 104
Kent, WA 98032–4429
Phone: 206–296–4280
E-mail: steven.davis@metrokc.gov
bk.palmer@metrokc.gov
http://www.metrokc.gov/sheriff

Lynnwood Police Department
High Tech Property Crimes
Det. Douglas J. Teachworth
19321 44th Avenue West
P.O. Box 5008 (mailing address)
Lynnwood, WA 98046–5008
Phone: 425–744–6916
E-mail: dteachworth@ci.lynnwood.wa.us
http://www.ci.lynnwood.wa.us/police/
  default.asp

Tacoma Police Department
Pierce County Data Recovery Unit
Det. Richard Voce
930 Tacoma Avenue South
Tacoma, WA 98402
Phone: 253–591–5679/253–594–7906
E-mail: rvoce@ci.tacoma.wa.us
http://www.TacomaPolice.org

Vancouver Police Department
Maggi Holbrook, CFCE
Computer Forensics Investigator
605 East Evergreen Boulevard
Vancouver, WA 98661
Phone: 360–735–8887
E-mail: ecrimes@ci.vancouver.wa.us
http://www.ci.vancouver.wa.us

**Washington State Department of Fish
and Wildlife**
John D. Flanagan
Computer Forensics Examiner
600 Capitol Way North
Olympia, WA 98501
Phone: 360–902–2210
Cell phone: 360–556–0195
E-mail: flanajdf@dfw.wa.gov
http://www.wa.gov/wdfw

Washington State Patrol
Computer Crimes Unit
Sgt. Keith Huntley
Supervisor
Airdustrial Way, Building 17
Olympia, WA 98507–2347
Phone: 360–753–3277
E-mail: khuntle@wsp.wa.gov

West Virginia

National White Collar Crime Center
1000 Technology Drive, Suite 2130
Fairmont, WV 26554
Phone: 877–628–7674
http://www.cybercrime.org

Wisconsin

Green Bay Police Department
Lt. Rick Dekker
307 South Adams Street
Green Bay, WI 54301
Phone: 920–448–3200
E-mail: rickdk@ci.green-bay.wi.us
http://www.gbpolice.org

Wisconsin Department of Justice
P.O. Box 7857
Madison, WI 53707–7857
Phone: 608–266–1221
http://www.doj.state.wi.us

Wood County Sheriff's Department
400 Market Street
Wis Rapids, WI 54495
Phone: 715–421–8700
E-mail: wcsd@tznet.com
http://www.tznet.com/wcsd

Wyoming

Casper Police Department
210 North David
Casper, WY 82601
Phone: 307–235–8489
http://www.cityofcasperwy.com/services/
 police.html

Gillette Police Department
Sgt. Dave Adsit, CCNA
201 East Fifth Street
Gillette, WY 82716
Phone: 307–682–5109
E-mail: davea@www.ci.gillette.wy.us
http://www.ci.gillette.wy.us

Green River Police Department
Corp. Tom Jarvie/Sgt. David Hyer
50 East Second North
Green River, WY 82935
Phone: 307–872–0555
E-mail: tjarvie@cityofgreenriver.org
dhyer@cityofgreenriver.org
http://www.cityofgreenriver.org/police/

Natrona County Sheriff's Office
Investigator Chris Poldervaart
201 North David Street
Casper, WY 82601
Phone: 307–235–9282
E-mail: poldc@natrona.net

Wyoming Division of Criminal Investigation
316 West 22nd Street
Cheyenne, WY 82002
Phone: 307–777–7183
Fax: 307–777–7252
Patrick Seals, Special Agent
E-mail: pseals@state.wy.us
Michael B. Curran, Special Agent
E-mail: mcurra@state.wy.us
Flint Waters, Special Agent
E-mail: fwater@state.wy.us
Bob Leazenby, Special Agent
E-mail: rleaze@state.wy.us
http://www.attorneygeneral.state.
 wy.us/dci

International

Australia

Western Australia Police
Det./Sgt. Ted Wisniewski
Computer Crime Investigation
Commercial Crime Division
Level 7 Eastpoint Plaza
233 Adelaide Tce
Perth WA 6000
Phone: +61 8 92200700
Fax: +61 8 92254489
E-mail: Computer.Crime@police.wa.gov.au

Brazil

Instituto De Criminalística - Polícia Civil Do Distrito Federal
SAISO - Lote 23 - Bloco "C" Complexo de Poilcia Civil
70610–200
Brasilia, Brazil
Phone: 55 +61 362–5948/55
 +61 233–9530
E-mail: perint@pcdf.df.gov.br

Canada

Royal Canadian Mounted Police
Technical Operations Directorate
Technological Crime Branch
1426 St. Joseph Boulevard
Gloucester, Ontario
Canada KIA OR2
Phone: 613–993–1777

Switzerland

Computer Crime Unit (GCI)
Det. Pascal Seeger/Det. Didiser Frezza
5, ch. de la Graviere
1227 Acacias, Geneva
Switzerland
Phone: +41 22 427.80.16 (17)
Fax: +41 22 820.30.16
E-mail: gci@police.ge.ch

United Kingdom

HM Inland Revenue
Special Compliance Office
Forensic Computing Team
Barkley House
P.O. Box 20
Castle Meadow Road
Nottingham
NG2 1BA
UK
Phone: +44 (0)115 974 0887
Fax: +44 (0)115 974 0890
E-mail: lindsay.j.scrimshaw@ir.gsi.gov.uk

National High-Tech Crime Unit
P.O. Box 10101
London
E14 9NF
UK
Phone: +44 (0) 870–241–0549
Fax: +44 (0) 870–241–5729
E-mail: admin@nhtcu.org

Appendix G. Training Resources List

The following list of nonprofit agencies, organizations, and institutions includes Federal, law enforcement, and academia sources that provide computer forensic training.

Arizona Regional Computer Forensic Laboratory
Sgt. R. Hopper
P.O. Box 6638
Phoenix, AZ 85005
Phone: 602–223–2698
Fax: 602–223–2332

Canadian Police College
P.O. Box 8900
Ottawa, Ontario
Canada K1G 3J2
Phone: 613–993–9500
E-mail: cpc@cpc.gc.ca
http://www.cpc.gc.ca

DoD Computer Investigations Training Program
911 Elkridge Landing Road
Airport Square 11 Building
Suite 200
Linthicum, MD 21090
Phone: 410–981–1604
Fax: 410–850–8906
E-mail: info@dcitp.gov
http://www.dcitp.gov

FBI Academy at Quantico
U.S. Marine Corps Base
Quantico, VA
Phone: 703–640–6131
http://www.fbi.gov/hq/td/academy/
  academy.htm

Federal Law Enforcement Training Center
Headquarters Facility
120 Chapel Crossing Road
Glynco, GA 31524
Phone: 912–267–2100
http://www.fletc.gov

Federal Law Enforcement Training Center
Artesia Facility
1300 West Richey Avenue
Artesia, NM 88210
Phone: 505–748–8000
http://www.fletc.gov

Federal Law Enforcement Training Center
Charleston Facility
2000 Bainbridge Avenue
Charleston, SC 29405–2607
Phone: 843–743–8858
http://www.fletc.gov

Florida Association of Computer Crime Investigators, Inc.
P.O. Box 1503
Bartow, FL 33831–1503
Phone: 352–357–0500
E-mail: info@facci.org
http://www.facci.org

Forensic Association of Computer Technologists
P.O. Box 703
Des Moines, IA 50303
Phone: 515–281–7671
http://www.byteoutofcrime.org

High Technology Crime Investigation Association (International)
1474 Freeman Drive
Amissville, VA 20106
Phone: 540–937–5019
http://www.htcia.org

Hilbert College
Economic Crime Investigation Program
5200 South Park Avenue
Hamburg, NY 14075
Phone: 716–649–7900
http://www.hilbert.edu

Information Systems Security Association (ISSA)
7044 South 13th Street
Oak Creek, WI 53154
Phone: 800–370–4772
http://www.issa.org

Institute of Police Technology and Management
University of North Florida
12000 Alumni Drive
Jacksonville, FL 32224–2678
Phone: 904–620–4786
Fax: 904–620–2453
http://www.iptm.org

International Association of Computer Investigative Specialists (IACIS)
P.O. Box 140
Donahue, IA 52746–0140
Phone: 877–890–6130
E-mail: iadmin@cops.org
http://www.cops.org

International Organization on Computer Evidence
Phone: +44 (0) 207–230–6485
E-mail: lwr@fss.org.uk
http://www.ioce.org

James Madison University
800 South Main Street
Harrisonburg, VA 22807
Phone: 540–568–6211
http://www.cs.jmu.edu/
  currentcourses.htm

Kennesaw State University
Southeast Cybercrime Institute
1000 Chastain Road
Kennesaw, GA 30144
Phone: 770–423–6965
http://cybercrime.kennesaw.edu

National Center for Forensic Science
University of Central Florida
P.O. Box 162367
Orlando, FL 32816–2367
Phone: 407–823–6469
E-mail: natlctr@mail.ucf.edu
http://www.ncfs.ucf.edu

National Criminal Justice Computer Laboratory and Training Center SEARCH Group, Inc.
7311 Greenhaven Drive, Suite 145
Sacramento, CA 95831
Phone: 916–392–2550
http://www.search.org

National High Tech Crime Training Centre
National Specialist Law Enforcement Centre
Wyboston Lakes Business and Leisure Centre
Great North Road
Wyboston, Bedfordshire
England MK44 3AL
Phone: +44 (0)01480 401872
Fax: +44 (0)1480 401950

National White Collar Crime Center
1000 Technology Drive, Suite 2130
Fairmont, WV 26554
Phone: 877–628–7674
http://www.cybercrime.org

Purdue University
CERIAS (Center for Education and
  Research in Information Assurance and
  Security)
Recitation Building
Purdue University
West Lafayette, IN 47907–1315
Phone: 765–494–7806
http://www.cerias.purdue.edu

Redlands Community College
Clayton Hoskinson, CFCE
Program Coordinator
Criminal Justice and Forensic Computer
Science
1300 South Country Club Road
El Reno, OK 73036–5304
Phone: 405–262–2552, ext. 2517
E-mail: hoskinsonc@redlandscc.net

University of New Haven
School of Public Safety and Professional
Studies
300 Orange Avenue
West Haven, CT 06516
Phone: 800–342–5864
http://www.newhaven.edu

**University of New Haven–California
Campus**
Forensic Computer Investigation Program
6060 Sunrise Vista Drive
Citrus Heights, CA 95610
http://unhca.com

U.S. Department of Justice
Criminal Division
Computer Crime and Intellectual Property
  Section (CCIPS)
10th and Constitution Avenue N.W.
John C. Keeney Building, Suite 600
Washington, DC 20530
Phone: 202–514–1026
http://www.cycbercrime.gov

Utica College
Economic Crime Investigative Institute
1600 Burrstone Road
Utica, NY 13502
Phone: 508–247–9504
http://www.ecii.edu

**Wisconsin Association of Computer
Crime Investigators**
P.O. Box 510212
New Berlin, WI 53151–0212
http://www.wacci.org

Appendix H. List of Organizations

The following is a list of organizations to which a draft copy of this document was mailed.

Alaska Criminal Laboratory
American Bar Association
American Society of Law Enforcement Trainers
Anchorage, Alaska, Police Department
Arapahoe County, Colorado, Sheriff's Office
Association of Federal Defense Attorneys
Bridgeport, Michigan, Forensic Laboratory
Bureau of Justice Assistance
Canadian Police Research Center
Cleveland State College Basic Police Academy
Commission of Accreditation for Law Enforcement Agencies
Connecticut Department of Public Safety
Criminal Justice Institute
Dallas County District Attorney's Office
Drug Enforcement Administration Computer Forensics
Fairbanks, Alaska, Police Department
Federal Bureau of Investigation
Federal Law Enforcement Training Center
Florida Department of Law Enforcement
Florida Department of Law Enforcement– Jacksonville Regional Operations Center
Florida Office of Statewide Prosecution
Frederick County, Maryland, State's Attorney's Office
Georgia Bureau of Investigation
Harlingen, Texas, Police Department
Illinois State Police
Indiana State Police Laboratory
Institute for Intergovernmental Research

Institute of Police Technology and Management
Institute for Security Technology Studies
Internal Revenue Service, Criminal Investigations
International Association of Chiefs of Police
International Association for Identification
Joint Council on Information Age Crime
Juneau, Alaska, Police Department
LaGrange, Georgia, Police Department
Law Enforcement Training Institute
Maine State Police Crime Laboratory
Massachusetts State Police Crime Laboratory
Metro Nashville Police Academy
Metro Nashville Police Department
Middletown Township, New Jersey, Police Department
MITRE Corporation
National Advocacy Center
National Aeronautics and Space Administration, Office of Inspector General, Computer Crimes Division
National Association of Attorneys General
National CyberScience Center
National District Attorneys Association
National Law Enforcement and Corrections Technology Center–Rocky Mountain
National Law Enforcement and Corrections Technology Center–Southeast
National Law Enforcement Council
National Sheriff's Association
National White Collar Crime Center
Naval Criminal Investigative Service
New Hampshire State Police Forensic Laboratory
North Carolina Justice Academy

Office of the District Attorney General–
Nashville, Tennessee
Office of Law Enforcement Technology
Commercialization
Ohio Bureau of Criminal ID and
Investigation
Orange County, California, Sheriff's
Department–Forensic Science Services
Orange County, New York, Community
College–Criminal Justice Department
Peace Officers Standards and Training
Pharr, Texas, Police Department
Regional Computer Forensic Laboratory
(San Diego, California)
Sedgwick County, Kansas, District
Attorney's Office
Sitka, Alaska, Police Department
Social Security Administration–Office of
the Inspector General
State of Florida Crime Laboratory
TASC, Inc.

Tennessee Bureau of Investigation
Tennessee Law Enforcement Training
Academy
Texas Rangers Department of Public
Safety
Town of Goshen, New York, Police
Department
U.S. Army Criminal Investigation
Laboratory
U.S. Attorney's Office–Western District of
New York
U.S. Department of Justice–Computer
Crime and Intellectual Property Section
U.S. Department of Justice–Fraud Section
U.S. Department of Justice–Office of
Overseas Prosecutorial Development
U.S. Department of Justice–Western
District of Michigan
Virginia State Police Academy

About the National Institute of Justice

NIJ is the research, development, and evaluation agency of the U.S. Department of Justice. The Institute provides objective, independent, evidence-based knowledge and tools to enhance the administration of justice and public safety. NIJ's principal authorities are derived from the Omnibus Crime Control and Safe Streets Act of 1968, as amended (see 42 U.S.C. §§ 3721–3723).

The NIJ Director is appointed by the President and confirmed by the Senate. The Director establishes the Institute's objectives, guided by the priorities of the Office of Justice Programs, the U.S. Department of Justice, and the needs of the field. The Institute actively solicits the views of criminal justice and other professionals and researchers to inform its search for the knowledge and tools to guide policy and practice.

Strategic Goals

NIJ has seven strategic goals grouped into three categories:

Creating relevant knowledge and tools

1. Partner with State and local practitioners and policymakers to identify social science research and technology needs.
2. Create scientific, relevant, and reliable knowledge—with a particular emphasis on terrorism, violent crime, drugs and crime, cost-effectiveness, and community-based efforts—to enhance the administration of justice and public safety.
3. Develop affordable and effective tools and technologies to enhance the administration of justice and public safety.

Dissemination

4. Disseminate relevant knowledge and information to practitioners and policymakers in an understandable, timely, and concise manner.
5. Act as an honest broker to identify the information, tools, and technologies that respond to the needs of stakeholders.

Agency management

6. Practice fairness and openness in the research and development process.
7. Ensure professionalism, excellence, accountability, cost-effectiveness, and integrity in the management and conduct of NIJ activities and programs.

Program Areas

In addressing these strategic challenges, the Institute is involved in the following program areas: crime control and prevention, including policing; drugs and crime; justice systems and offender behavior, including corrections; violence and victimization; communications and information technologies; critical incident response; investigative and forensic sciences, including DNA; less-than-lethal technologies; officer protection; education and training technologies; testing and standards; technology assistance to law enforcement and corrections agencies; field testing of promising programs; and international crime control.

In addition to sponsoring research and development and technology assistance, NIJ evaluates programs, policies, and technologies. NIJ communicates its research and evaluation findings through conferences and print and electronic media.

To find out more about the National Institute of Justice, please visit:

http://www.ojp.usdoj.gov/nij

or contact:

National Criminal Justice
 Reference Service
P.O. Box 6000
Rockville, MD 20849–6000
800–851–3420
e-mail: *askncjrs@ncjrs.org*

www.ingramcontent.com/pod-product-compliance
Lightning Source LLC
Chambersburg PA
CBHW081828170526
45167CB00007B/2753